Foreword .

In 1998 the Government set a target for 60 percent of new homes in the UK to be built on previously developed land (brownfield sites).[1] A significant proportion of this land is likely to be affected by contamination, much of it as a result of former industrial uses, rendering it unsuitable for redevelopment without remedial treatment.

This policy will mean that for many developers, dealing with contamination will become commonplace, rather than the exception to the rule. The first results of the National Land Use Database (NLUD) project,[2] published in 1999, indicate that there is an opportunity to build over 400,000 dwellings on brownfield sites which are already vacant or derelict.

This report has been published to promote the adoption of good practice in the identification, investigation, assessment and remedial treatment of land affected by contamination. Adoption of good practice will ensure that development for housing can be undertaken safely and with confidence that no unacceptable risks remain.

Dr J. Pentreath
Chief Scientist
Environment Agency

Acknowledgements

This report is based in part on draft reports, on development of housing on land affected by contamination prepared by Parkman Ltd., in contract with the Department of the Environment, Transport and the Regions. The contributions by Parkman and the Department are gratefully acknowledged.

The preparation of the report (which was jointly sponsored by the Environment Agency and the NHBC), was overseen by a Project Board, consisting of representatives of the Environment Agency, NHBC and the Department of the Environment, Transport and the Regions.

Contents

Box 1.1 Definitions of Contaminated Land

A commonly used and simple definition of contaminated land is *"land which contains potentially harmful substances as a result of human activity"*. This includes land which, while potentially harmful, is not of immediate concern. It excludes hazards from naturally occurring substances. Pollution, as distinct from contamination, may be defined as *"the presence of a potentially harmful substance as a result of human activity in sufficient concentration or amount as to cause harm or to be highly likely to cause harm"*. This definition can apply to other media, in addition to land. To classify land as polluted, therefore, requires us to take into account land use and other factors. An assessment is therefore required to test whether contamination is causing or is likely to cause harm or pollution.

The above definition is similar to that adopted for contaminated land by NATO/CCMS[6] in 1989, which was *"land that contains substances that when present in sufficient quantities or concentrations are likely to cause harm directly or indirectly to humans, the environment or on occasions to other targets"*. This definition introduced the concept of targets, more commonly referred to as receptors. It recognised that harm can be caused to a range of receptors and not just humans.

The Department of the Environment, in its consultation paper "Paying for Our Past",[7] issued in 1994, defined contaminated land as *"land which, because of its former use, now contains substances that present hazards likely to affect its proposed form of development, and which requires an assessment to determine whether the proposed development should proceed or whether some form of remedial action is required"*. This definition recognises the need not only for assessment to determine the condition of the land but also for remedial action to manage unacceptable risks and to render the land suitable for its proposed use.

Part IIA of the Environmental Protection Act[3] gives a new statutory definition of contaminated land, which is land that *"appears to the local authority in whose area it is situated to be in such a condition, by reason of substances in, on or under the land, that significant harm is being caused or there is a significant possibility of such harm being caused; or pollution of controlled waters is being, or is likely to be caused"*. Statutory guidance states how such land is identified and the steps necessary to secure its remediation.

All the above definitions are based explicitly or implicitly on the concept of harm or pollution. Part IIA of the Environmental Protection Act[3] defines "harm" as *"harm to the health of living organisms or other interference with the ecological systems of which they form a part, and in the case of man includes harm to his property"*. It is clear, therefore, that land which is not "contaminated land" under Part IIA of the Environmental Protection Act[3] may contain substances with the potential to cause harm if the land use is changed. Therefore, any land which may contain potentially harmful substances should be subject to a formal risk management process prior to its development for housing to ensure that the risks are managed and that it is suitable for its intended use. This requirement applies just as much to land containing naturally high levels of harmful substances as it does to land contaminated by past human activity. It also applies to existing development where contamination is discovered which could render the land unsuitable for its current use.

---

exposed to the contamination (such as through direct skin exposure to contaminated soil or ingestion of contaminated water or contaminated vegetables grown in the soil). The "source-pathway-receptor" concept is central both to the statutory definition and the broader concept of contaminated land as discussed in Box 1.

For the purposes of Part IIA, the term "source" is replaced by the term "contaminant" in this concept. A schematic representation of the concept is shown in Figure 1.1. Where a contaminant, a pathway and a receptor can be identified which relate to each other this is described in the statutory guidance[5] for Part IIA of the Environmental Protection Act as a pollutant linkage. This term refers here to any contaminant-pathway-receptor relationship in any context, and its use does not always imply that the Part IIA regime is applicable.

Receptors may be humans, animals or plants; they may also be part of the general environment, such as water resources, or they may be building structures and services, such as water mains or pipes. Certain pathways may also be receptors themselves, for example groundwater could act as a pathway for transporting contaminants to a distant receptor but may itself be affected and thus represent a receptor in its own right.

Whether a potential contaminant produces adverse effects on a receptor depends upon various factors, including:

- its concentration at source;

- the chemical, biological or physical availability of the contaminant which may be affected by the type of soil, the presence of water or other substances;

- the number and types of pathways and the fate and behaviour of the contaminants within the pathways;
- the length of exposure of a receptor to a contaminant;

- the sensitivity of receptors to the contaminant, for example the higher sensitivity of children to contaminants such as lead, because of their size, play habits and physiology compared with that of adults;

Source–pathway–receptor concept

- synergy, whereby two or more contaminants found together cause more harm than the sum of their effects taken separately;

- antagonistic effects, such that the harm by two or more contaminants found together can be much less significant than the sum of their effects taken separately.

Where the risk to a receptor is considered to be unacceptably high, the risk needs to be reduced, which normally means that remedial treatment will be required. However, the presence of a contaminant does not necessarily mean that there is a risk of harm to a receptor. The pollutant linkage must be established before the existence of an unacceptable risk can be confirmed.

Where land is being developed for residential use, examples of human receptors to be considered include:

- site investigation and construction workers or trespassers, for example children getting on to sites during redevelopment;

- the various occupants and users of land after its development, for example house occupiers, maintenance personnel;

- the various occupants and users of adjacent sites, whether used for residential or other purposes.

Table 1.1 gives examples of the mechanisms and exposure pathways by which contaminants may threaten human receptors, while Table 1.2 gives examples of environmental receptors.

Contaminants may attack materials in building components, leading to their weakening and ultimately to their possible

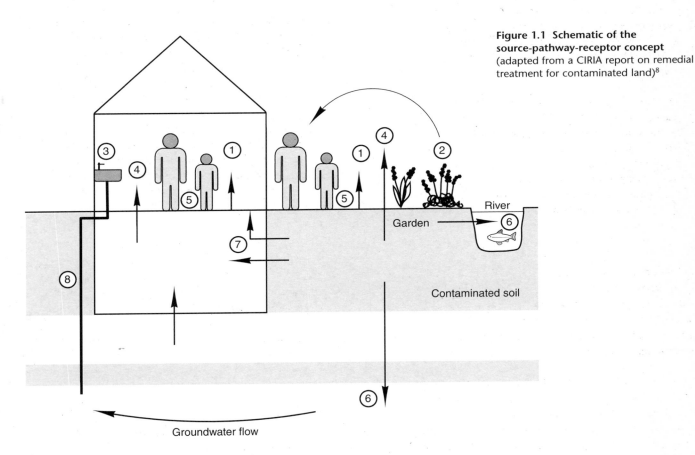

Figure 1.1 Schematic of the source-pathway-receptor concept (adapted from a CIRIA report on remedial treatment for contaminated land)[8]

Groundwater flow

possible pathways

Ingestion:	of contaminated soil/dust	①
	of contaminated food	②
	of contaminated water	③
Inhalation:	of contaminated soil particles/dust/vapours	④
Direct contact:	with contaminated soil/dust or water	⑤
Pollution of controlled waters		⑥
Attack on building structures		⑦
Attack on services		⑧

failure. The effect of sulphates on concrete structures is an example well known to the construction industry.[9] Other examples include contaminants passing through walls of water service pipes or causing degradation of pipework and affecting the taste or potability of water supplies, and the accumulation of gases creating potentially explosive or asphyxiant conditions.

Concern about contamination is not restricted only to land polluted by human activities, or by industrial uses, or by specific substances. Rather, it covers any substances or conditions that can cause harm, including gases such as methane and carbon dioxide, pathogenic organisms and naturally high levels of toxic substances, including radioactive substances. It is therefore possible that agricultural land and other apparently greenfield sites can also be contaminated.

The general principle governing the regulation of the development of contaminated land in the UK is that land should be suitable for its intended use and not pollute the surrounding environment. The approach to assessment therefore takes into account the sensitivity of the intended use to contamination. Where the proposed end use is housing, this

is invariably more sensitive to contamination than industrial or commercial uses. The redevelopment process can not only introduce new receptors, but it may also introduce new pathways or modify existing ones. Accordingly, it must never be assumed that a site is fit for redevelopment for housing merely because a previous owner has not been required to remediate it or there has been no regulatory action taken by the appropriate authorities. It may require remedial work to render it suitable for housing. Furthermore, even if a site has been remediated and as a result is not considered to be contaminated in its current state, it still may not be suitable for housing without further remediation. The remedial treatment required for many sites is therefore determined as much by the type of development proposed as by the environmental risks posed by the site in an undeveloped condition.

1.2.2 How does contaminated land arise?

Much of the land that is contaminated has been used for industrial or commercial activities involving use, manufacture or storage of substances that are toxic, harmful or polluting. Contamination of the land may have occurred through process leakage, from spillages in production and storage areas,

Table 1.1   Examples of mechanisms and exposure pathways for human receptors

Mechanism	Typical exposure pathways
Inhalation	Breathing dust and fumes (indoors and outdoors)
	Breathing gas emissions (indoors and outdoors)
Ingestion	Eating - contaminated soil, for example, by small children (outdoors) - plants grown on contaminated soil Ingesting dust or soil on vegetables Drinking contaminated water
Contact	Direct skin contact with contamination (particularly through wounds) in soil (outdoors) and dust (indoors)
	Direct skin contact with contaminated liquids

Table 1.2   Examples of environmental receptors for soil contamination

Receptor	Typical implications
Groundwater	Contamination leads to a restriction/prevention of use as a resource, for example, drinking water, and can have secondary impacts on other resources which depend on it (for example aquatic ecosystems, rivers whose baseflow is from groundwater).
Surface water (ponds, lakes, streams, rivers)	Contamination leads to a restriction/prevention of use: - as drinking water resource - for amenity use Effects on aquatic life.
Outdoor air	Deterioration caused by releases of dust/fumes/gases, for example, during construction.
Indoor air	Deterioration in quality caused by seepage of gases from contaminated ground into buildings.
Soil	Phytotoxic substances affecting ability to sustain plants.

4

through deliberate disposal of wastes onto or into the ground, from decommissioning of plant and demolition of buildings and from agricultural practices. Industrial accidents may also have caused the land to become contaminated.

Sites which have been used for processing or disposal of industrial and household wastes can be contaminated, for example through the natural degradation of waste materials. However, contamination is not confined to industrial and waste disposal sites. Other land may have become contaminated as a result of deliberate application of pesticides and herbicides, rather than accidental spillage or wastage of materials.

Land not previously used for any of the above activities may still become contaminated as a result of migration of contamination coming from other sites nearby. This could occur through movement or seepage of surface water or groundwater, movement of gases through the ground, dust deposition or migration along drains or service trenches.

Hazardous substances may be present as a result of natural processes. For example, methane can arise from peat deposits[10] and radon, a radioactive gas, may be emitted from certain geological formations.[11]

1.2.3 How much land is contaminated?

It has always been difficult to quantify the extent of contamination of land. This is partly because recognising and understanding the problem is a recent development, even though much of the problem began with the industrial revolution. The Urban Task Force Report[12] suggests that there are between 50,000 and 200,000 hectares of land affected by contamination in the UK. Some of this land will be potentially or actually harmful in its current state (that is without redevelopment) and much more of it will require remediation to render it suitable for redevelopment for sensitive uses, such as housing.

Many sites will have been contaminated by industrial activities during the twentieth century and earlier, for which records may have been destroyed or extremely difficult to unearth. Many sites will never have been investigated, despite having been through the redevelopment process previously. Consequently, when bringing forward a brownfield site for development it will often be the case that no site-specific information is available from the vendor or from the appropriate authorities.

1.2.4 What types of site may be contaminated?

An extensive list of the industrial uses of land that may have caused contamination is shown in Appendix 1. For each of the uses in Appendix 1 an Industry Profile[13] has been published by the (former) Department of the Environment. Each profile describes the industrial processes, materials used and produced and the contamination likely to have arisen from these.

Most contaminated land will have been subjected to one or more of the uses described in the *Industry Profiles*. However, some land will have been contaminated by other means such as fly-tipping or naturally occurring contamination. Consequently, if a development site has never been subjected to any of the uses listed in Appendix 1 it cannot be guaranteed free of contamination, but if it has been occupied by any of the listed uses developers should assume that it is contaminated unless further investigation or assessment indicates otherwise.

1.2.5 What types of contaminant may be present?

The Industry Profiles[13] identify substances known to be associated with each industrial use. For some uses there are over 100 such contaminants. The most important contaminants because of their frequency of occurrence and known harmful effects are shown in Appendix 1.

1.2.6 UK policy on contaminated land

UK policy[14] is based on the "suitable for use" principle for the control and treatment of existing contamination. This means that remediation is required where there are unacceptable risks to health or the environment arising from the actual or intended use of the site. The risk-based approach to management of contaminated land is described in more detail in Part 2 and forms the basis of the guidance.

Where land is being redeveloped, the developer will normally be responsible for the costs of any work necessary to make the land safe within the process of a successful and satisfactory development.

Under the new Part IIA regime, liability for the financial consequences of contamination rests with those who cause or knowingly permit it, in accordance with the "polluter pays principle". However, in some cases the polluter cannot be found and the landowner may be responsible.

This policy provides a basis for tackling real hazards where they exist, while avoiding the imposition of unnecessary financial and regulatory burdens. It seeks to encourage the adoption of reasonable means to achieve remedial objectives, striking a balance between the costs of remediation and the environmental benefits it creates. It is intended to lead to greater certainty and confidence in the market, helping to ensure that contaminated land is brought back into productive use.

1.3 KEY ISSUES FOR HOUSING DEVELOPMENT ON CONTAMINATED LAND

1.3.1 Key issues for new and existing housing

In July 1998 the UK Government announced a policy target that 60 percent of new housing should be constructed on brownfield sites. Government policy on planning for housing has been set out in a revised Planning Policy Guidance note (PPG3).[1] Since 3.8 million new homes are expected to be required by 2021, the policy target suggests that some 2.2 million will be built on such sites. Brownfield sites are those that have been subject to some previous development or use, and a significant proportion of these is likely to be contaminated. Much, but by no means all, of the contamination has arisen from former industrial uses of land. Greenfield sites, in contrast, are those that have never been developed, but some of them may have been contaminated as a result of former uses for agriculture and through naturally present substances.

Government policy aims to promote the regeneration of urban areas while reducing development pressure in the countryside. It is carried through by local planning authorities and by various agencies, including the Regional Development Agencies, the Environment Agency for England and Wales and the Scottish Environment Protection Agency (SEPA) for Scotland.

1.3.2 Commercial and financial issues

1.3.2.1 Sale and purchase or transfer of land and property

The availability and quality of information on contamination is extremely important for the sale and purchase or transfer of land and property. Sellers will wish to avoid misrepresentation and may need information to support the guarantees, warranties and indemnities that are increasingly being sought by purchasers to protect themselves from the financial consequences of unforeseen or undiscovered contamination.

A new development may lead to enquiries about contamination by potential purchasers, their legal advisers and lenders. Purchasers may be concerned about their health and safety when living in a house as well as the long-term saleability of the property. Lenders may be concerned about property value as a means of security for a loan. Increasingly, solicitors and conveyancing agents are becoming aware of contamination issues and may obtain information on potential contamination through local searches. Where this is the case, prospective purchasers will wish to be assured that the contamination has been dealt with in an appropriate way and that the relevant authorities have been involved. Transparency about the information held on a site and the reasons for decisions about contamination is very important to an effective commercial market in contaminated land. Initiatives such as the Ministerial Task Group's proposals[15] in 1999 for a voluntary scheme under which sellers of residential property would provide a seller's information pack in order to speed up transactions may help to promote such transparency.

Statutory guidance[5] under Part IIA of the Environmental Protection Act[3] describes how liabilities for contamination under the Act relate to transactions in land and/or property which may be contaminated.

1.3.2.2 Insurance

Use of the structured risk-based approach now adopted in the UK has stimulated the development of financial products which mitigate financial risk associated with contamination. These products are generally insurance-based. They can provide cover/finance of the following kinds which could benefit housebuilders:

- cover against risk of residual contamination causing harm;

- indemnity cover (where indemnities or warranties are required as part of a sale and purchase agreement);

- stop loss cover on costs of remedial treatment;

- annuity schemes for remedial treatment;

- risk financing.

Products that go with the land and are therefore transferable to purchasers are likely to be of particular interest, especially where they are divisible. This, for example, would make it possible for a developer to obtain cover for an entire development site, divisible into separate policies for each individual property when sold.

The contamination risk cover now introduced by NHBC into its "Buildmark" policy (see section 1.4.2) protects home owners and occupiers against specified contaminated land liabilities.

Developers and builders should note that many insurance and finance-based solutions are bespoke for individual sites and depend on a detailed audit of development proposals and of contaminated land risk assessment. Submission of assessment reports prepared in accordance with this guidance is likely to assist in securing cover quickly and at reasonable premiums, while proposals based on inadequate assessment are unlikely to be insurable at reasonable cost, if at all. Insurers will also want confidence in the remedial work carried out, its validation and long-term effectiveness.

1.3.3 Communication of contamination issues

Sites being brought forward for development will not generally be isolated from the community. Contaminated sites are often located adjacent to existing housing, schools or leisure facilities. Some contaminated sites may be used informally by the community for recreational purposes. Indeed, it will often be found that members of the public living or working near development sites will have important information or opinions relating to contamination. Where existing development is found to be affected by contamination, those living in such developments will be particularly concerned about the risks of direct exposure to the contamination. Developers, builders and regulatory authorities alike will therefore have to plan carefully how they anticipate and respond to community concerns and anxieties. These concerns are sometimes based on perceptions inconsistent with objective scientific or engineering judgement. Nevertheless, they should be taken seriously and treated with sensitivity.

In general, nothing will be gained by attempting to conceal from concerned parties the nature, extent and response to contamination on site. The passing of new legislation and the activities of local authorities and the environment agencies in tackling contamination are likely to stimulate increased public awareness of the issues. Much can therefore be gained by adopting a policy of communication of information to the community and responding to the feedback received.

A good communication policy will be based on establishing and maintaining trust. Community stakeholders must be involved in discussions as early as possible and responsiveness to their views must be demonstrated. Developers should therefore take the trouble to explain complex issues and demystify technical terminology so that they do not cause alarm to the community. Developers should also advise the community in advance of any activities on site that may cause alarm unless carefully explained beforehand. For example, the adoption of protective clothing by workers on site as a general precaution might be misinterpreted by local residents that they are at risk of exposure to harmful substances.

Further guidance on communication issues is provided in a handbook produced by the Scotland and Northern Ireland Forum for Environmental Research (SNIFFER) on communicating understanding of contaminated land risks.[16]

1.3.4 Obtaining specialist advice

Specialist advice is essential to deal effectively with the multidisciplinary problems of developing a site affected by contamination, and will need to be obtained from elsewhere if it is not available to the developer within his/her own organisation.

Guidance on the procurement and delivery of contaminated land consultancy services is provided in a Department of the Environment, Transport and the Regions Contaminated Land Research Report (CLR12) on quality assurance in contaminated land consultancy.[17] Specialist consultants can assist developers in:

- identifying and characterising contaminated land;

- designing and implementing investigations;

- estimating and evaluating environmental and health risks;

- providing specific health and safety advice in relation to activities on site, particularly during the investigation and construction phases;

- designing and supervising remedial actions;

- liaising with regulatory bodies, the community and others on the developer's behalf.

Many consultancies which have contaminated land expertise employ a range of specialists to cover a number of issues. These might include chemists, ecologists, geotechnical engineers, hydrogeologists, health and safety advisors (including planning supervisors as required by the Construction Design and Management Regulations) and planning specialists.

The CLR report on quality assurance in environmental consultancy[17] provides information about listings and directories of consultancies and identifies professional bodies and trade associations whose members provide contaminated land services. It also provides practical advice on selecting, briefing and engaging specialists and includes examples of technical briefs and forms of agreement that might be used.

1.4 THE REGULATORY FRAMEWORK

1.4.1 The planning regime

When considering development proposals, planning authorities are obliged to ensure that all material planning considerations, which can include the actual or possible presence of contamination[69], are satisfactorily addressed. The Town and Country Planning (General Permitted Development) Order (GPDO)[18] sets out which organisation must be consulted for specific types of development or for development in specific areas. The organisations which must be consulted are called statutory consultees. For example, where a housing development requires the construction of new roads or involves a forecast increase in traffic, the local highways authority must be consulted. Where development is to take place within 250 m of the boundary of a landfill site the appropriate environment agencies must be consulted. Planning authorities can also consult with other organisations and take into account their comments. Sections 1.4.1.1 to 1.4.1.4 and 1.4.2, describe the roles of the principal consultees who may be asked to comment on contamination issues.

The developer may be able to use the consultation process to obtain valuable background information on matters such as contamination, building solutions already applied in the locality and planning permissions and records of planning conditions applied to land used for a similar purpose to the site under consideration.

1.4.1.1 The planning authority

Planning authorities are responsible for regulating development and land use in the public interest. They have extensive powers to halt or reverse development carried out in the absence of relevant permissions or in contravention of planning conditions. Planning authorities have the power to require the developer to provide such further information as is needed to determine an application for planning permission, and may ask for reports on investigation of contamination. Planning officers will take advice on contamination issues from the relevant environment agency (section 1.4.1.2), local environmental health officers (section 1.4.1.3), the Health and Safety Executive (section 1.4.1.4) and building control officers (section 1.4.2.1), as necessary.

In addition to the planning permission normally required for new buildings or change of use, a project where contaminated land is involved may require planning permission if any of the following conditions apply:

● there is on-site disposal of controlled waste;

● there is on-site remedial treatment;

● engineering works are to be carried out as part of the remedial treatment;

● treatment is part of a development for which planning permission is required; or

● ground investigation works are to be carried out.

Where the planning authority identifies specific measures to be undertaken, these requirements can be imposed either by conditions attached to the planning permission or by means of planning agreements under Section 106 of the Town and Country Planning Act.[19] Examples of conditions or agreements designed to take account of specific measures are:

● specific remedial treatment to the site, such as removal or treatment of all materials with contaminant concentrations above stated levels;

● alteration of the design of the development to eliminate particularly sensitive uses such as gardens, or to rezone areas to relatively less sensitive uses, for example by substituting public open space for private gardens;

● a programme of monitoring to check that remedial measures have met and continue to meet acceptance criteria.

The Town and Country Planning General Permitted Development Order[18] grants deemed planning permission for a wide range of certain types of development which are therefore immune from planning control under the Town and Country Planning Act.[19] Where such permitted development could be inappropriate in relation to contamination, local authorities can withdraw deemed planning permission in relation to specific areas or types of development using a so-called "Article 4 direction". This could be used, for example, to

prevent activities that could breach cover systems (for example excavation for swimming pools) or could introduce new risks (such as the construction of garden sheds on land that could be affected by gas emissions where the main development is protected from those emissions).

Since the imposition of conditions is a common means of securing safe development, it will normally be in a developer's interest to contact the planning authority at an early stage to avoid delays when it considers the planning application.

1.4.1.2 The environment agencies

The Environment Agency was formed by the Environment Act 1995 from the National Rivers Authority (NRA), Her Majesty's Inspectorate of Pollution (HMIP), the waste regulation authorities and sections of the Department of the Environment). It is a statutory consultee in England and Wales under the planning process on the matters for which it has regulatory responsibility. These include protection of the water environment, flood defence and waste management. In the context of developments on contaminated land, the Agency advises planning authorities on applications where pollution of surface water or groundwater is involved, or where the water environment might be at risk of pollution as a result of the development. The Agency also advises on applications proposing development close to or on landfill sites and within flood-plain areas.

The Agency also has wider roles in disseminating good practice, advising the Government, undertaking research and development and promoting development of sustainable technologies for remedial treatment. It may support local authorities in this respect also.

In Scotland, the Scottish Environment Protection Agency (SEPA) was established under the Environment Act (1995). In the context of contaminated land matters, SEPA is responsible for functions equivalent to those of the Environment Agency in England and Wales.

In Northern Ireland the Department of the Environment Northern Ireland is responsible for most of the environmental regulation, including the protection of surface and groundwaters. Although, the Environment Act 1995 does not specifically apply to Northern Ireland, similar provisions are provided by Part 3 of the Waste and Contaminated Land Order 1997, which is yet to be implemented through regulations.

1.4.1.3 Local authority environmental health functions

Local authority environmental health officers are responsible for protecting public health. They provide advice to their planning authorities on technical matters relating to contaminated land including the discharge of planning conditions and on liaison matters with the environment agencies. Environmental health officers will be concerned with people's health and safety both on and off site, and ensuring that the development proceeds in accordance with any contaminated land-related planning condition or Section 106 agreement. They are responsible for ensuring that activities within their jurisdiction do not give rise to a "statutory nuisance", including matters such as smoke, noise, odours, dust and "any accumulation or deposit which is prejudicial to health".

Under Part IIA of the Environmental Protection Act[3] , local authorities are the lead regulator for contaminated land. They and the environment agencies have specific duties in relation to prevent harm or pollution from contaminated land. Following implementation of Part IIA, the statutory nuisance provisions will no longer apply to contaminated land where it is prejudicial to health because regulatory responsibility will pass to local authorities and the environment agencies under the Contaminated Land Regulations.

1.4.1.4 The Health and Safety Executive (HSE)

The HSE is responsible for the enforcement of the Health and Safety at Work Act[20] and associated regulations, designed to protect the safety of workers in the workplace or others who may be at risk of harm as a result of workplace activities. The HSE has published advice on the protection of workers and the general public during the development of contaminated land. In the context of development, a planning supervisor appointed under the Construction Design and Management Regulations[21] is likely to be required to inform the HSE of construction processes (including demolition and ground improvement) at contaminated sites.

1.4.2 Building and development control

The Building Regulations[22] ensure the health and safety of people in and around buildings by providing functional requirements for building design and construction. In addition, the regulations promote energy efficiency and contribute to meeting the needs of the disabled. Builders and developers are required to obtain building control approval which requires an independent check that the development is in compliance with the regulations. There are two types of building control providers, the local authority and approved inspectors.

Building Regulations[22] stipulate that building work complies with the detailed requirements of the regulations. Contamination is covered by Requirement C2 which states that precautions should be taken to avoid danger to health and safety caused by substances found on or in the ground to be covered by a building. Whenever contamination is suspected it is a statutory requirement for the local environmental health function to be consulted. Contamination is also relevant to Requirement A, concerning the structural integrity of buildings.

1.4.2.1 Local authority building control functions

Local authority building control functions may be involved throughout construction in enforcing the building regulations. Early consultation with the relevant officers is advisable. Building control records may themselves be useful sources of information about previous design solutions and remedial treatment applicable to the site in question or its surroundings.

1.4.2.2 NHBC

The National House-Building Council (NHBC) was set up over 60 years ago as the standard-setting and independent regulatory body for the UK house-building industry. NHBC exists to help registered builders to build better homes and to offer insurance and consumer protection for house purchasers. It is a non-profit distributing organisation, governed by an independent council, representing the interests of a range of stakeholders. Approximately 150,000 new homes built by 19,000 registered builders are registered with NHBC annually. In April 1999, NHBC extended its Buildmark warranty to provide cover for stated contaminated land liabilities. NHBC has been designated as an approved inspector since 1985 and is able to grant approval under the Building Regulations throughout England and Wales.

1.4.3 Part IIA of the Environmental Protection Act 1990[3]

Part IIA of the Act defines contaminated land as land which "appears to the local authority in whose area it is situated to be in such a condition, by reason of substances in, on or under the land, that significant harm is being caused or there is a significant possibility of such harm being caused; or pollution of controlled waters is being, or is likely to be caused". Statutory guidance describes regulatory responsibilities for identifying contaminated land and securing its remediation.

Having identified contaminated land, local authorities and the environment agencies must decide whether sites identified by the former as contaminated land under the regime are Special Sites. The forthcoming Contaminated Land Regulations will describe which land will fall into this category. The regulatory responsibilities for Special Sites fall to the environment agencies. In general, Special Sites will be those where the agencies are best placed to be the enforcing authority, either because the land is likely to cause particular difficulties in which the agencies have expertise, or because the agencies have an existing regulatory role and it is sensible for this to encompass contamination issues.

The statutory guidance makes clear that the Part IIA regime applies to the current condition of land. It may therefore be directly applicable to existing housing on land that meets the statutory definition of contaminated land. Whichever body is the regulator under Part IIA, they are obliged to ensure that remediation is carried out, wherever possible by the appropriate person, rather than using public money. An appropriate person is one who has caused or knowingly permitted substances to be in, on or under the land which render it contaminated. Such a person is responsible under Part IIA for remediation of the land. Where, after reasonable inquiry, no person can be found to bear responsibility under this criterion, the owner or occupier for the time being of the contaminated land is an appropriate person. Developers and builders therefore need to be aware that, in some circumstances, they could be liable for the remediation.

The control of remediation and redevelopment of contaminated land for new housing is, and will remain after implementation of Part IIA, primarily the responsibility of local planning authorities and will continue to be handled under the existing planning system. However, in order for the land to be redeveloped successfully the minimum requirement is that it is remediated to the degree necessary to render it uncontaminated with respect to the definition in the Act, so that there is no unacceptable risk under its intended use. Thus, for all practical purposes, the technical assessments of whether land can be classified as "contaminated" are also likely to be applied to the assessment of proposals for redevelopment of land which may be contaminated.

If existing housing is built on Part IIA contaminated land causing significant harm to health, it is likely that the Director of Public Health will be involved. The Health and Safety Executive may be involved in any remediation work carried out under the Part IIA regime, as described in section 1.4.1.4.

1.4.4 Other regulatory regimes

In addition to their role as a statutory consultees under the planning regime on matters for which they have regulatory responsibility, the environment agencies also have direct regulatory authority for waste management activities. These are covered by the Waste Management Licensing Regulations 1994.[24] They issue and maintain registers of waste management licences and certificates of exemption, enforce conditions of licences and determine whether licences can be surrendered. Where developers are proposing that material from a contaminated site is redeposited or treated on site, the agencies will advise on whether the activity requires a waste management licence. Many remedial activities which involve treating contaminated soils and groundwater fall within the scope of the waste management licensing regime. Spreading of waste soil on some types of land may be exempted from licensing, but these activities must be registered with the relevant environment agency so that they can be controlled.

The environment agencies also regulate discharges to controlled waters (for example rivers and streams) for which authorisation is required. These usually stipulate that discharges should be free of polluting matter, but may also set limits on the concentrations of specific substances with a requirement to monitor and report the quality of the discharge.

Where groundwater is polluted, but there is no "pollutant linkage" to existing land contamination, the Environment Agency in England and Wales has the powers under Section 161A of the Water Resources Act 1991 to serve a "works notice". This may be served to ensure that pollution of controlled waters is remediated by the party who caused or is knowingly permitting the pollution to occur.

The Environment Agency has issued interim guidance on classification of contaminated soils for the purposes of disposal at licensed waste facilities.[25]

Part 2. Guidance on the UK approach to safe development of housing on land affected by contamination

2.1 BACKGROUND

In common with many other countries, the UK approach to managing contaminated land is risk-based. Risk management principles underlie the legislative requirements of Part IIA of the Environmental Protection Act[3] and the "suitable-for-use" approach used in other contexts such as planning and development control. The approach is founded on the concept of the contaminant-pathway-receptor relationship, or pollutant linkage. The purpose of remediation of contaminated land is therefore to break pollutant linkages, for example by removing or treating the contaminant (for example, by excavation of contaminated material), removing or blocking the pathway (for example, by isolating the source beneath protective layers or installing barriers to prevent migration) or removing or protecting the receptor (for example, by changing the form or layout of development).

In adopting this approach each site must be subject to an individual risk assessment because the sensitivity of the intended use in the case of housing and the nature of pollutant linkages will depend on the following three factors:

● the design and layout of the development;

● whether or not it has gardens and, if so, where they are situated;

● what materials and precautions will be used in construction.

The risk is also influenced by factors such as the nature of the contamination, its location, the quantities or concentrations present, the physical and chemical properties of the soil and the bioavailability of the contaminant. For this reason there are no prescriptive limits, standards or guideline values for contaminant concentrations that must be achieved on all development sites irrespective of the type of development. Instead, there are ranges of values from which appropriate site-specific criteria are selected, depending on the nature of the development or the intended use of the site.

The risk-based approach is the basis of the Model Procedures[4] which are described in section 2.2.

2.2 THE MODEL PROCEDURES

The approach to managing contamination issues for housing development is based on guidance in the *Model Procedures for the Management of Contaminated Land*.[4] That document provides details of the structured approach to management of contaminated land in a number of contexts. It also provides a useful guide to professionals on the content, organisation and structure of documentation required to support the approach.

The Model Procedures describe the process of dealing with contaminated sites and in particular how to make appropriate decisions with respect to risk estimation and evaluation, selection of remedial measures and implementation of risk management action. The process involves first identifying objectives for the work, obtaining information, making decisions and taking action based on the decisions made. Setting objectives is key to making best use of resources and information. For housing development key objectives typically include:

● ensuring that the development is "suitable for use";

● providing information to support financial decisions;

● providing information to support decisions on sale or acquisition of land or properties ;

● providing information for insurance purposes;

● satisfying regulatory requirements;

● avoiding potential regulatory action;

● working within programme and budget constraints, for example for investigation.

The three primary procedural stages described in the Model Procedures[4] are covered in sections 2.2.1 to 2.2.3 of this guidance. The procedural stages have been translated into a sequence of steps summarised in sections 2.2.1 to 2.2.3 of this guidance and described in detail in sections 2.5 to 2.8.

2.2.1 Risk assessment

The model procedure for risk assessment describes the activities where the risks to human health or the environment which may be associated with contamination are identified, estimated and evaluated. Within the procedure, there are two phases. Phase 1 includes two sub-stages (phases 1a and 1b) covering initial data gathering and preliminary evaluation:

● hazard identification, typically involving desk studies and site reconnaissance to obtain sufficient information on the site to gain a preliminary understanding of the potential risks (this equates to steps 1 and 2 of this guidance);

● hazard assessment involving refining the understanding of the risks, primarily by confirming the likelihood of suspected pollutant linkages, sometimes as a result of

2.3 PRACTICAL STEPS FOR HOUSING

In the context of housing development, the Model Procedures[4] have been translated into a series of practical steps. These cover all the activities from initial enquiry to completion of remedial works, shown in Figure 2.1. All steps apply to both new and existing development.

● The steps should be followed in sequence. This is essential for four important reasons:

● a site with no obvious environmental problems, and which appears suitable for its current use may not be automatically suitable for housing;

● if contamination is not addressed at the outset, dealing with it can be costly when development is already under way;

● responsibility for collection and review of all the information needed about contamination on a site rests with the developer rather than the regulatory authorities, although the latter will often be able to provide some information;

● each step in the guidance depends on the findings of the previous step, such that if a step is omitted it is possible that the entire management process and hence the development itself could be compromised.

The last of these is of particular importance. As a rule, at the beginning of each new step a review of the information provided by previous steps should be undertaken and documented to ensure that there is a sufficient basis for continuing. The Model Procedures[4] emphasise that an iterative approach is an important aspect of good practice in the management of contaminated land. Although each step in the guidance is presented as a discrete entity, it is often the case that a review of information obtained indicates the need to go back to earlier steps in order to obtain more data or make a reassessment. In this way, a picture of the contamination on a site and the appropriate methods for dealing with it is built up in a phased approach.

The practical steps shown in Figure 2.1, on which this guidance is based, are:

● gathering of information about the site to determine its industrial past or discover other uses or location-specific factors that might have led to contamination and to obtain other physical information such as the known geology and hydrogeology in the area (step1);

● identification of contaminants associated with former uses of the site or its geographical location and the development of a list of those to be investigated (step 2);

● identification of receptors which could be at risk from exposure to contaminants (steps 1-3);

● identification of pathways through which exposure could occur (steps 1 - 4);

● development of a conceptual model based on plausible pollutant linkages (steps 3 and 4);
● design and execution of the ground investigation and analysis including refinement of the conceptual model (step 5);

● evaluation of the significance of the levels of contaminants found and their locations in the context of the proposed development and the development of remedial objectives (steps 6 and 7);

● selection of a remedial strategy for the development (steps 8 and 9);

● design, implementation and verification of risk management action, including submission of plans, reports and proposals for approval, design and execution of the remedial works (step 10);

● implementation of monitoring and maintenance programmes (Step 11);

● completion and filing of all relevant documentation (all steps);

● consultation with appropriate advisory and regulatory authorities at key stages throughout the process.

Consultation is recommended at several stages throughout the development process. The local planning authority will be responsible for determining the planning application. Since land contamination is a material planning consideration, the authority will often consult the relevant environment agency and its own environmental health officers and may impose planning conditions relating to the issue of contamination. It is beneficial to consult the various authorities and agencies involved in the early stages of the process. The connection between the process followed by the developer in dealing with contamination issues and the planning process for new developments is also shown in Figure 2.1

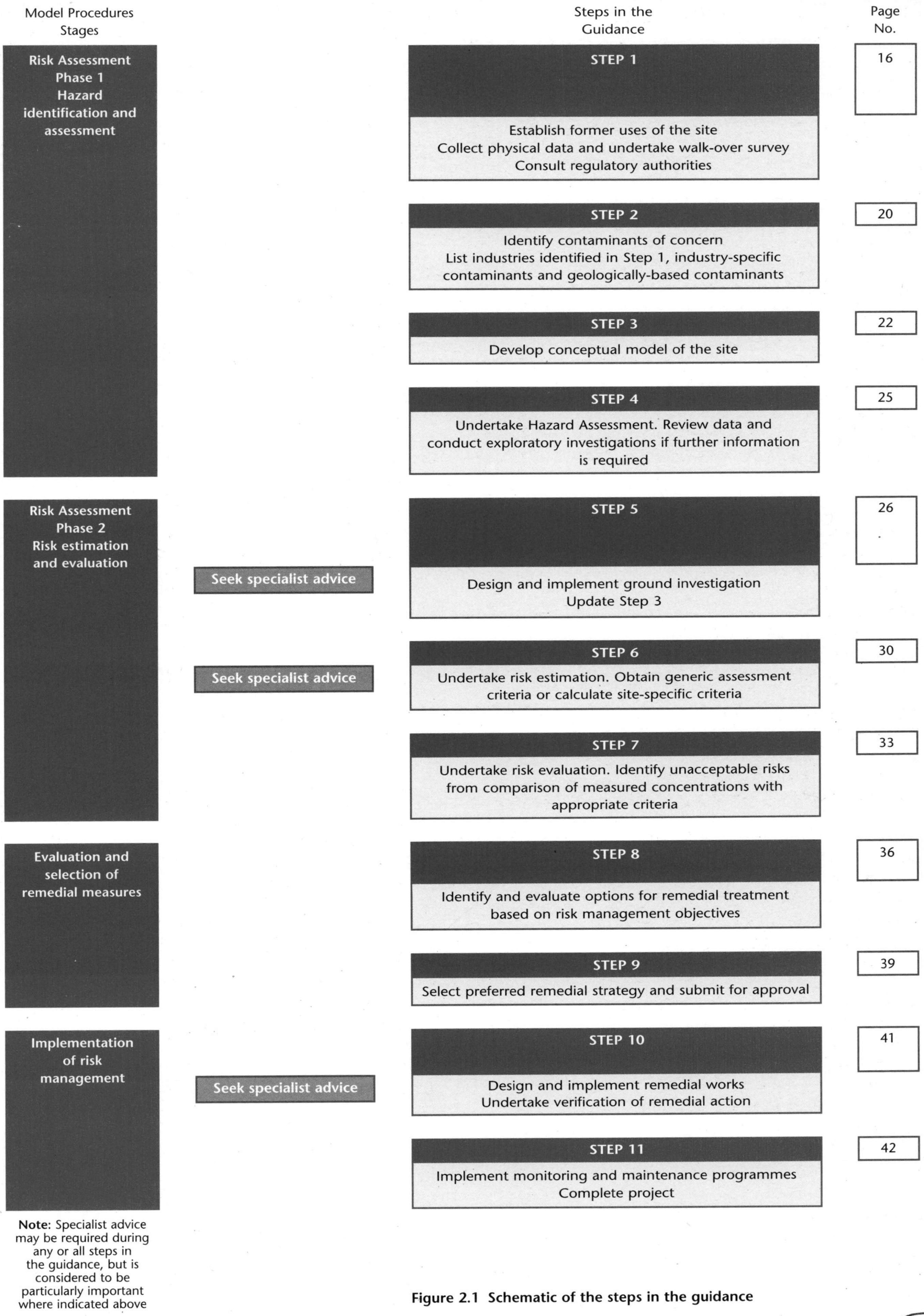

Model Procedures Stages	Steps in the Guidance	Page No.

Model Procedures Stages		Steps in the Guidance	Page No.
Risk Assessment Phase 1 Hazard identification and assessment		**STEP 1** Establish former uses of the site Collect physical data and undertake walk-over survey Consult regulatory authorities	16
		STEP 2 Identify contaminants of concern List industries identified in Step 1, industry-specific contaminants and geologically-based contaminants	20
		STEP 3 Develop conceptual model of the site	22
		STEP 4 Undertake Hazard Assessment. Review data and conduct exploratory investigations if further information is required	25
Risk Assessment Phase 2 Risk estimation and evaluation	Seek specialist advice	**STEP 5** Design and implement ground investigation Update Step 3	26
	Seek specialist advice	**STEP 6** Undertake risk estimation. Obtain generic assessment criteria or calculate site-specific criteria	30
		STEP 7 Undertake risk evaluation. Identify unacceptable risks from comparison of measured concentrations with appropriate criteria	33
Evaluation and selection of remedial measures		**STEP 8** Identify and evaluate options for remedial treatment based on risk management objectives	36
		STEP 9 Select preferred remedial strategy and submit for approval	39
Implementation of risk management	Seek specialist advice	**STEP 10** Design and implement remedial works Undertake verification of remedial action	41
		STEP 11 Implement monitoring and maintenance programmes Complete project	42

Note: Specialist advice may be required during any or all steps in the guidance, but is considered to be particularly important where indicated above

Figure 2.1 Schematic of the steps in the guidance

2.4 DOCUMENTATION

A fundamental requirement of good practice for dealing with land contamination is that complete and accurate documentary records are prepared and maintained throughout the progress of managing the site. The importance of this becomes apparent when submission of plans and applications is being considered. All the parties involved will wish to see clear, detailed and unambiguous reporting on all issues relating to contaminated land. Increasingly, developers can expect that reports on contamination will be assessed by reference to the growing body of established good practice as set out in authoritative guidance documents such as the Model Procedures[4] and this guidance document.

The process of obtaining information must therefore be approached in a systematic way. Developers should be aware that while gaps in the documentary record do not necessarily invalidate documentation as a whole, the regulatory bodies are likely to have less confidence in the information provided. As a principle, therefore, it is recommended that the reasons for any gaps in the information are clearly stated.

KEY REPORTS ARE:

- preliminary (desk study and walkover survey) reports;

- site investigation and risk assessment reports;

- remedial strategy and remedial options reports, design details and method statements;

- post remediation reports, including records of as-constructed work and verification;

- environmental monitoring reports.

Additionally, other reports may also be developed as part of compliance with statutory requirements and the overall management of the site, including:

- health and safety files, maintained by the planning supervisor in accordance with the provisions of the Construction Design and Management Regulations;[21]

- report on tenders for remedial works;

- procurement or contractual information including terms or deeds of appointment, warranties, insurance details, etc.;

- contract progress reports for remedial works;

- waste management licence application and working plan.

A checklist of typical documents that would be prepared for a housing development on land affected by contamination is shown in Appendix 3.

2.5 RISK ASSESSMENT PHASE 1 – HAZARD IDENTIFICATION AND ASSESSMENT

This section covers steps 1-4 of the guidance, which describe risk assessment phase 1, involving hazard identification and assessment. These steps are shown schematically in Figure 2.2, together with the link to the subsequent steps in risk assessment phase 2, when risks are estimated and evaluated. Sections 2.5.1 to 2.5.4 describe these steps in more detail.

STEP 1

2.5.1 – establish former uses of the site and collect other background information

2.5.1.1 Overview

In this step, information is gathered to establish whether a site could be contaminated, the key contaminants involved and other physical factors which could affect their behaviour. This information is used to determine the nature of any risks associated with contamination which could influence the choice of remedial treatment.

The activities in this step are applicable to both new and existing development. On existing developments, awareness that contamination may be an issue can arise in several ways, including:

- information obtained as a result of the process of sale or transfer of land or property;

- discovery of new information on site history;

- discovery during investigations or works for upgrading or refurbishing of property;

- investigation of actual or potential health problems or pollution incidents;

- regulatory action in relation to Part IIA of the Environmental Protection Act 1990.

The details covered in this step are:

- identification of previous and current site usage;

- collection of physical information about the site;

- identification of potential receptors;

- site visit and walkover;

- consultation with authorities.

2.5.1.2 Identification of previous and current site usage

It is essential to find out whether the site or surrounding land has ever accommodated any of the industrial uses listed in Appendix 1, any other potentially contaminative uses not listed

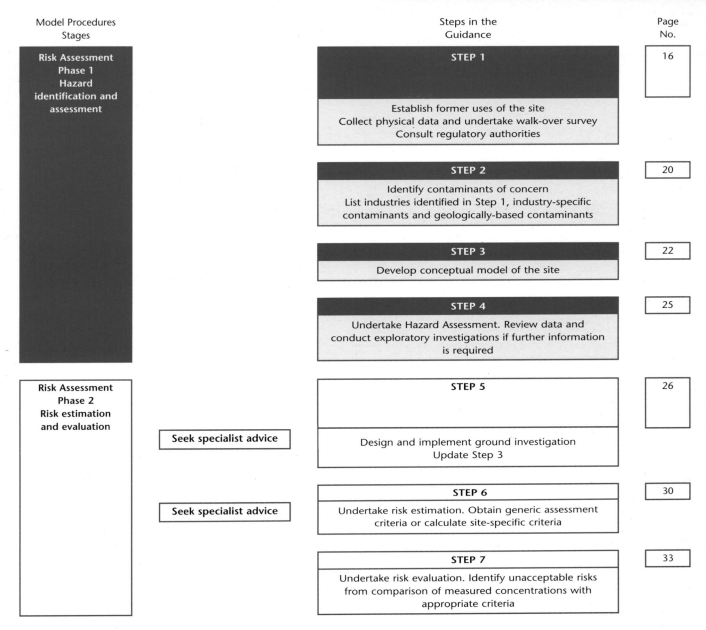

Figure 2.2   Steps in risk assessment phase 1 – hazard identification and assessment

in Appendix 1 (such as mining), or whether there is any other reason to suspect contamination. There are numerous sources of such information, including local libraries, for example for maps and local historical publications, local authorities, other regulators, national archives such as those maintained by the British Geological Society, and public directories. Sources of information are described in more detail in a CLR report on documentary research on industrial sites.[29] Several companies now supply summaries of archived data (such as copies of maps, records of boreholes, indications of adjacent and nearby uses, etc.) on a commercial basis. This can be a very cost-effective means of gathering data quickly. However, you should ascertain the source and provenance of data before deciding what level of reliance to place upon it.

The most obvious of the former uses of the site will be its most recent use, if known. Many sites will have had several previous uses, however, of which the current owners or occupiers may

be unaware. Former uses are most readily established by a search of old maps and street directories. Older Ordnance Survey maps provide a wealth of detail about the uses of land by industry, but some of this detail is lost in later years. For example, a site which would have been shown as a "chemical works" or "soap factory" at the turn of the century may simply be labelled "works" on more recent series. Street directories and property registers may provide missing detail.

Detail can often be filled in from local authority records. The Land Registry can provide details of former owners from which potential contaminative uses may be deduced. The planning authority will also have records of planning applications. The environmental health function may have records of industrial processes where these have been regulated under the local authority air pollution control provisions of the Environmental Protection Act. The relevant environment agency may also have useful records.

2.5.1.3 Collection of physical information about the site

The significance of contamination on a site and the risks posed by it can be affected very significantly by certain physical factors, such as geology, hydrogeology, geotechnical factors and topography. Where certain physical conditions are encountered, you may need further information or to take particular care. Examples of such conditions are given in table 2.1, together with a commentary on their implications. These factors should also be taken into account in developing the conceptual model (step 3). In some cases it may be appropriate to take specialist advice, for example if unidentifiable stockpiles or containers of suspect material are found.

For all situations involving controlled waters (for example within flood plains, overlying aquifers or close to rivers, streams or lakes), the appropriate environment agency should be consulted.

Where landfills identified from step 1 lie within approximately 250 m of the site boundary it indicates a risk of landfill gas and leachate migration into the site. Where these sites are active or subject to aftercare under a waste management licence, regulatory authorities will have more information and should be consulted.

2.5.1.4 Identification of potential receptors

At an early stage in the process of investigating land that may be affected by contamination it is important to identify receptors that could be at risk of exposure to contaminants. Potential receptors include:

- future occupants of the planned housing development or occupants of an existing development;

- occupants of neighbouring land and developments;

Table 2.1   Physical characteristics which may indicate that particular care is required

Characteristics	Commentary
Where groundwater could affect or be affected by construction, including: – trenches for services/drains – infilled areas – foundations and piling.	Ground investigation will need to take account of water sampling and testing requirements. Advice from specialists on the design of ground investigations and applicability of remedial measures in any given situation is required.
Where the site may be subject to flooding.	Flooding may result in the mobilisation of contaminants and migration into "treated" areas which may prejudice the effectiveness of remedial works already undertaken. This should be considered in the risk assessment.
Where surface water features are situated within 500m of the site boundary.	Land topography, discharges and drainage from the site may result in potentially contaminated discharges to surface water, especially during works on site.
Where poor geotechnical conditions, for example loose fill, mining, solution cavities, are identified.	All circumstances where potential ground instabilities may occur require advice from a geotechnical specialist.
Where landfills are situated within 250m of the site.	Landfills may generate methane and carbon dioxide (see Waste Management Paper 27) which should be identified as potential contaminants for the ground investigation.
If made ground is encountered, especially where the depth is greater than 3-4m.	Extent and nature of made ground may not necessarily be identified via trial pits. Deeper boreholes may be required.
Where there is undulating topography at site boundary.	Additional risk of run off with lateral contaminant movement from the site to neighbouring land, or on to the site from adjacent land with history of potentially contaminative uses.
Existence of material of uncertain origin for example stockpiles, drums or "coloured" materials.	These may contain contaminants in concentrated form. Contents of containers may not match the descriptions on labels.
Where the site borders sensitive land uses such as land under tree preservation orders.	Land use may not be conducive to treatment action that may cause damage for example, to trees.
Where services/conduits pass into neighbouring land.	These could provide pathways to create pollution linkages with receptors on adjacent land, requiring specific attention at site boundaries.

- the general public, where they have access to an unsecured site;

- workers on the site, including those involved in preliminary walkover surveys;

- watercourses on or adjacent to the site;

- groundwater below and around the site;

- natural features on and adjacent to the site (such as ponds, woodland), especially where these may have conservation value or have statutory protection.

2.5.1.5 Site visit and walkover

CLR 2 provides guidance on preliminary site inspection on contaminated sites.[30] When entering a potentially contaminated site for the first time the risk of exposure to the

Table 2.2   Information exchanges during the planning consultation process

Information supplied by:		Commentary
The developer/specialist adviser	Regulatory authorities	
Documentary information on potentially contaminating activities, ground conditions in locality and development layout planning		Provides basis for establishing with the relevant environment agency and local authority the extent of any necessary physical land investigation, including the range of contaminants and type of investigation
Design principles for foundations and surface water drainage, for example sewers, drains, outfalls, ponds, soakaways, ditches		Provides information for identifying possible causes for concern in protection/penetration into underlying aquifers. Building control issues may also be raised by local authority
Proposals for ground investigation		To establish extent of information to be supplied. Special measures may be required when drilling is proposed through suspected contaminated material into aquifers.
	Groundwater quality	Environment agencies can provide water quality data and risk assessment which may assist in design of foundations, construction and protection of services.
	Instances of flooding	Environment agencies can provide data for development planning/design.
	Abstraction licence information	Environment agencies may provide information on source protection zones and water abstraction points which may then be identified as vulnerable to contamination. Specialist advice needed.
	Discharge consent information	Environment agencies may identify discharges which could affect the site or provide guidance on constraints which may then be applied to any future application to discharge. Specialist advice needed to interpret data.
	Water quality information	Surface water and groundwater information from environment agencies may indicate current levels of contamination in controlled waters.
	Records of pollution incidents	May indicate whether a pollution incident has arisen on-site or whether neighbouring sites have been polluters of controlled waters. Specialist advice needed to interpret data.
	Groundwater vulnerability	Environment agencies give information on sensitivity of underlying strata. Specialist hydrogeological advice needed to interpret data.
Outline planning proposals, including reclamation, layouts, surface treatments, drainage		May indicate whether planning conditions should be attached to planning consents and means by which they may be discharged.

contamination should be considered and appropriate health and safety precautions should be taken. In addition to normal site wear (hard hat and appropriate footwear), protective gloves should be used if any material is to be handled. Dusty areas should be avoided or entered only if face masks are used. Confined spaces may contain poisonous or asphyxiant gases and should be approached very cautiously. In general, brownfield sites are likely to be much more hazardous than greenfield sites and special precautions should be undertaken. Details of these are beyond the scope of this guidance. However, useful information is produced by the Health and Safety Executive[31] and CIRIA.[32]

A site visit may yield information from the inspection of the exterior of the site and from a detailed reconnaissance (walkover). Where a site is derelict, some idea about its former use can be obtained if drums or packages of raw materials or products remain on the site. A walk-over can also reveal whether fly-tipping of waste has occurred and whether this could lead to potential contamination that would not be identifiable purely from archive data. Other visible indications of contamination include soil or water discoloration, subsidence, stressed vegetation, odours and liquid discharges from the ground.

The neighbours can often provide very valuable information about former activities, perhaps providing the names of companies that operated on the site or individuals formerly associated with it. Even anecdotal information can be of value when forming initial views about a site.

2.5.1.6 Consultation with authorities

An initial consultation with the regulatory and planning authorities may reveal information relevant to the risk assessment process. They may comment on potential impacts of contamination on controlled waters, they may advise on specific issues to be addressed, for example where these fall outside the scope of this guidance, or they may provide specific advice on the additional information or reports that they would wish to see. Typical information that may be provided to or requested from the authorities is provided in Table 2.3.

At the end of this step it should be possible to state whether or not the site has had a former industrial use or uses and, if so, to identify those with one or more Industry Profiles[13] listed in Appendix 1. This will allow the potential contaminants on the site to be identified (step 2). This information also feeds into the development of a conceptual model of the site in the context of the proposed development (step 3).

STEP 2

2.5.2 – identify contaminants of concern

2.5.2.1 Overview

This step involves compiling a site-specific list of all contaminants of concern. This involves listing:

- each known current or former industrial use of the land;

- the key contaminants corresponding to each industrial use listed in Appendix 1;

- other contaminants known to be associated with the relevant industrial uses, where these are suspected;

- other contaminants known or suspected to be present from the walkover survey;

- potentially harmful substances which may occur naturally in the locality;

- substances or soil characteristics which may affect the behaviour and therefore the risk estimates for listed contaminants.

2.5.2.2 Identification of contaminants from industrial uses

The list of key contaminants associated with each industrial use of land known or suspected at the site would form the basis for identifying contaminants of concern. Any specific substances identified during the site walkover should also be added. Key contaminants associated with industrial uses of land as described in the Industry Profiles are shown in Appendix 1.

It should be noted that Appendix 1 does not list all contaminants identified in each Industry Profile[13].

However, if the presence of a substance not listed in Appendix 1 but included in the relevant Industry Profile is suspected or known to be present from historical records it should be added to the list of contaminants of concern.

2.5.2.3 Identification of contaminants from other sources

The list of contaminants of concern should also include any substances which may occur naturally in the locality, such as radon, a radioactive gas emitted from a range of rocks, or gases emitted from natural organic deposits, such as peat or coal measures, which can generate methane and carbon dioxide.

Since estimates of risk for many contaminants found on industrial sites depend on the soil pH and concentration of soil organic matter, these should also be added to the list. Where guideline values have been published for particular contaminants these will indicate whether they are influenced by soil factors such as organic matter or pH.[26] However, these factors can represent contamination in their own right. Very high levels of organic matter might indicate a risk of anaerobic decay to produce methane and carbon dioxide. They may also indicate that the ground is combustible and that there may be a fire risk. Extremes of pH indicate the presence of acids or alkalis. Variation of pH and organic matter will also be important when considering the risks that soil contaminants pose to the water environment.

Table 2.3   Contaminants for which special care may be required during investigation or handling of contaminated material

Contaminant*	Reason for specialist advice	Action * See Appendix 4 for additional information.
Drummed contaminants	Uncertainty of contents (do not rely on descriptions on labels).	Seek specialist advice (see Table 2.1).
Liquid contaminants	Remedial measures to cope with liquids are beyond the scope of this guidance.	Seek specialist advice.
Metals: beryllium, cadmium, silver, mercury, thallium, arsenic, vanadium, lead, Cr.	Significant toxicity.	Seek specialist advice prior to work on site to interpret significance of presence and take precautions to avoid exposure of site workers.
Organics: aromatic hydrocarbons aliphatic halocarbons, aromatic halocarbons, chlorophenols, acetone	Wide range of compounds, with complicated toxicities and related effects. Sample collection and testing requirements may be complex. Many of these substances are more mobile than metals and inorganics.	Seek specialist advice prior to ground investigation if presence is suspected from review of land uses. Seek specialist advice to interpret significance of presence.
dioxins/furans	Significant toxicity.	Seek specialist advice prior to ground investigation if presence is suspected from review of land uses.
asbestos	Risk to site workers/occupiers. Particular risk from airborne fibres. Identification of types of asbestos usually undertaken by specialists.	Seek advice prior to ground investigation if presence is suspected from review of land uses. Seek advice on prevention of fibre release.
carbon dioxide Methane	Gases which can migrate over long distances. Methane explosion risk. Risk to site workers of asphyxiation. Housing design modifications may be required.	Seek advice prior to ground investigation if presence is suspected from former uses or landfill is identified within 250m of site.
Oxygen depletion	Risk to site workers of asphyxiation.	Prevent working in confined spaces
Loss on Ignition / Calorific value	Significance of presence and design solutions.	Seek advice if generic assessment or site-specific criteria are exceeded.
Radioactivity	Exceptional and complex health and safety risks.	Seek specialist advice before entering site if presence is suspected from review of land uses.
Explosives and munitions	Range of substances and complexity of potential implications.	Seek specialist advice prior to entering site if presence is suspected from review of land uses.
Pathogens	Exceptional health and safety risks.	Seek specialist advice prior to entering site if presence is suspected from review of land uses.
Pesticides	Range of substances and related toxicity. Risk to site workers.	Seek specialist advice prior to ground investigation.

When certain contaminants are expected, special precautions might be required. Examples of such contaminants are shown in Table 2.3, with indications of the reasons for seeking advice. These include extremely toxic substances, highly mobile liquids and gases and complex mixtures. Some of these substances are likely to be hazardous to workers on site during the site reconnaissance and investigative stages of development, so it is important to obtain advice before site work starts.

The list of contaminants of concern with respect to the proposed development of the site is taken forward to the development of the conceptual model in step 3.

STEP 3

2.5.3 – develop a conceptual model

2.5.3.1 Overview

In this step, information obtained during steps 1 and 2 of this guidance is used to develop a conceptual model of the site. The conceptual model is based on the potential pollutant linkages identified for the site. It is a representation in summary form of the nature of the contamination problem for which a solution is being sought. It can be expressed in a tabular, matrix or pictorial format.

The activities in this step are applicable to both new and existing developments. For new developments, the conceptual model will reflect conditions before detailed investigations commence and will be updated to reflect the progression through each step of the guidance to completion of the development and risk management actions. For existing developments, the conceptual model will reflect the current situation and may be based on quite different pathways and receptors from those that would be relevant for a development site.

2.5.3.2 Identifying components of the conceptual model

The conceptual model should identify:

● each of the receptors (for example occupants of the development, neighbours, controlled waters), breaking these down into separate categories where appropriate (for example separate identification of adults and children, groundwater and surface water);

● the pathways by which they could be exposed (for example inhalation or ingestion of contaminated soils or dust, consumption of home-grown vegetables affected by contamination, leaching of contaminants into groundwater);

● the contaminants associated with former uses of the site or thought likely to be present;

● a preliminary assessment of the likelihood of a pollutant linkage for each combination of contaminant, pathway and receptor.

An example of a simple, preliminary conceptual model in tabular format is shown in Table 2.4. The main groups of sensitive receptors for a range of key contaminants are shown in Table 2.5. An example of a pictorial representation of a conceptual model is shown in Figure 2.3, which shows possible routes of entry of gas into a dwelling.

The conceptual model is central to the development of any site affected by contamination. It summarises the nature of the problem for which a solution is being sought. The conceptual model determines the way in which subsequent stages of the guidance are followed, and ensures that each relevant pollutant linkage is investigated fully. It must therefore be kept fully up

to date as risk assessment, selection of remedial measures and implementation of risk management proceed.

2.5.3.3 Updating the conceptual model

The first version of the conceptual model is relevant for the design and implementation of the ground investigations. The information obtained from the investigations would be used to check and update the conceptual model. For example, a model based on risk of exposure of occupants of future development to contamination in soil by direct contact would need to be modified if during ground investigation waste deposits capable of producing landfill gas were to be encountered. The risks associated with accumulation of gases in confined spaces would then need to be considered. Further investigations of gas concentrations in the ground might be required, and the data from these may result in further amendments to the conceptual model to reflect a new pollutant linkage.

The conceptual model might also be updated if the form of the proposed development is changed. For example, on a development incorporating private gardens that could be cultivated by residents for vegetables the conceptual model could include identification of toxic heavy metals to which residents could be exposed by eating contaminated produce. On a site with no private gardens and managed public open space, consumption of vegetables grown in contaminated soil may not be a relevant pollutant linkage.

Further versions of the conceptual model would be prepared prior to beginning of the construction phase. During this phase, linkages could be different to those of concern prior to commencing the ground investigation. The final model would be prepared to represent the situation on completion of the risk management action.

Table 2.4. Example of a preliminary conceptual model of pollutant linkages (adapted from the Model Procedures[4])

Substances			Pathway	Receptor
X	Y	Z		
✓	✓	✓	Ingestion and inhalation of contaminated soil and dust	Human health
?[1]	?[1]	✓	Uptake into home-grown produce	
✓	✓	✓	Surface water run-off into surface waters	Water environment
?[2]	?[2]	✓	Migration through ground into surface or groundwater	
?[1]	?[1]	✓	Vegetation on site growing in contaminated soil	Flora and fauna
✓	✓	✓	Aquatic life in affected waters	
x	x	x	Contact with contaminated soil	Building materials

Key: ✓ - pollutant linkage likely   ? - pollutant linkage possible
x - pollutant linkage unlikely   1 - depends on soil pH
2 - depends on leaching characteristics

Table 2.5 Key contaminants on industrial land and sensitive receptors

Concomitants	Receptor group				
Group	Contaminant	Humans (human health)	Vegetation and the ecosystem	Construction materials	Water
Metals	Cadmium	✔	✔		✔
	Chromium	✔	✔		✔
	Copper		✔		✔
	Lead	✔	✔		✔
	Mercury	✔	✔		✔
	Nickel	✔	✔		✔
	Zinc		✔		✔
	Beryllium	✔			✔
	Vanadium	✔	✔		✔
	Silver	✔	✔		✔
	Thallium	✔			✔
Metalloids	Arsenic	✔			✔
	Barium	✔	✔		✔
	Selenium	✔	✔		✔
	Boron		✔		
	Cyanide	✔	✔	✔	
	Nitrate				✔
	Sulphate		✔	✔	✔
	Sulphide		✔	✔	
	Sulphur	✔	✔	✔	✔
	Ammonium	✔		✔	✔
	Chloride			✔	
Organics	Fuel/Hydrocarbons	✔	✔	✔	✔
	PAH	✔			✔
	Phenol	✔	✔	✔	✔
	Aromatic hydrocarbons	✔	✔	✔	✔
	Aliphatic hydrocarbons	✔	✔	✔	✔
	Aromatic halocarbons	✔	✔	✔	✔
	Aliphatic halocarbons	✔	✔	✔	✔
	Chlorinated phenols	✔	✔	✔	✔
	Pesticides/herbicides	✔	✔		✔
	Dioxin/furans	✔	✔		✔
	Organometallics	✔	✔		✔
	PCB	✔	✔		✔
	Acetone	✔	✔		✔
Others	Asbestos	✔			
	PH	✔	✔	✔	✔
	Carbon dioxide	✔	✔		
	Methane	✔	✔		
	Explosives	✔	✔	✔	✔
	Radioactivity	✔	✔		
	Radon	✔	✔		
	Pathogens	✔	✔		✔

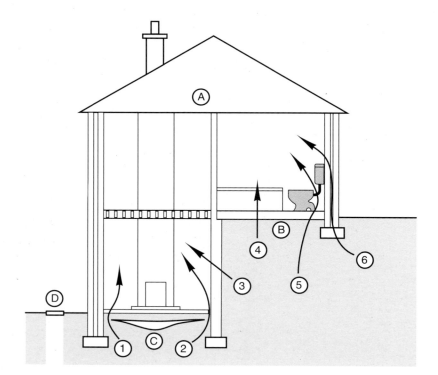

Figure 2.3 Conceptual model of gas entry into a building[8]

Key to ingress routes:

① Through cracks and openings in solid concrete ground slabs due to shrinkage/curing cracks
② Through construction joints/openings at wall/foundation interface with ground slab
③ Through cracks in walls below ground level possibly due to shrinkage/curing cracks or movement from soil pressures
④ Through gaps and openings in suspended concrete or timber floors
⑤ Through gaps around service pipes/duct
⑥ Through cavity walls

Locations for gas accumulations:

Ⓐ Wall cavities and roof voids   Ⓒ Within settlement voids
Ⓑ Beneath suspended floors   Ⓓ Drains and soakaways

STEP 4

2.5.4 – undertake Hazard Assessment

2.5.4.1 Overview

The main objective of this step is to re-evaluate the initial conceptual model developed in Step 3. This is done in order to:

- establish the likelihood of each of the potential pollution linkages;

- address the nature, likely location and behaviour of contaminants;

- identify potential for chronic and short-term health risks.

2.5.4.2 Review of information

The first task in this step is to critically evaluate all data collected so far and assess any further data collection needs. In some cases there may be a need for further information before phase 2 of the risk assessment can be attempted. The Model Procedures[4] indicate that these additional activities may not always be necessary and that development of the conceptual model (step 3) and stage 2 (risk estimation and evaluation) may be undertaken without them. In order to obtain additional information it may be necessary, for example, to undertake some exploratory investigations prior to the more comprehensive ground investigations undertaken as part of the risk estimation in phase 2.

The review should identify potential health and safety implications of exploratory investigations and set out appropriate protective measures for workers on site. It should also address the potential environmental implications of carrying out investigations. When contaminated material is disturbed, for example through excavation of trial pits or drilling of boreholes, new pathways can be introduced which could put a range of receptors at risk. For example, drilling through contaminated soil into groundwater could introduce a new migration pathway for contaminants to be washed down into the aquifer.

2.5.4.3 Exploratory investigations

Such investigations should be undertaken to confirm the existence of the hazards suspected from the earlier desk study and site walkover. They should also give an indication of the likely quantities of contaminants present and their probable locations. The design of investigations is covered in more detail in step 5 (section 2.6.1).

The results of exploratory investigations are used to update and refine the conceptual model. For each pollutant linkage, the location of the source, likely quantity or concentration of contaminant, and existence of pathways can be confirmed. This then allows a preliminary indication of the nature and magnitude of risks to be made.

2.6 RISK ASSESSMENT PHASE 2 – RISK ESTIMATION AND EVALUATION

The practical steps covering risk estimation and evaluation are highlighted in Figure 2.4, below and are discussed in sections 2.6.1 to 2.6.3 of this guidance.

STEP 5

2.6.1 – design and implement ground investigation

2.6.1.1 Overview

In this step detailed investigations of the site are designed and undertaken. The purpose of detailed investigations is to produce sufficient information about the locations, concentrations and behaviour of contaminants to undertake risk estimation and evaluation (see Step 6 and subsequent steps).

The quality of data about the site conditions, including the validity of the results of sampling soil, water and gases critical to a risk assessment. Developers may therefore wish to take specialist advice on the design and implementation of investigations. When planning an investigation in nearly all cases it will be necessary to commission analysis from a suitably qualified and experienced laboratory (see section 2.6.1.3). This can be done directly or through a consultant. In many cases, the ground investigation itself will be undertaken by a specialist contractor, whose services can be procured directly or indirectly through a consultant. Guidance on the selection of service providers is given in CLR 12[17]. Appendix 5 gives a list of professional bodies, trade associations and listing agencies who may be able to supply lists of service providers. The decision to appoint a specialist consultant or contractor must be based on the level of competence and experience held by the developer.

Typically, detailed investigations would produce the following information:

- the locations of contaminated zones within the site;

- types and concentrations of contaminants in soil and groundwater;

- concentrations and flows of gases such as carbon dioxide and methane;

- other physical and chemical characteristics of soil and groundwater that can influence the behaviour of the contaminants, such as pH, organic matter, soil porosity and water levels.

The details covered in this step are:

- design of the investigations;
- investigation techniques;

- analysis of samples;

- uncertainty;

- typical costs.

2.6.1.2 Design of investigation

The output from steps 1 to 3 will provide information on the former uses of the site, and the important contaminants associated with each. Initial consultations with the relevant authorities will have revealed any additional concerns about contamination that may not have been identifiable from archive material or from a visual inspection of the site. At this stage a list of the contaminants for which assessment is required will also have been produced.

The ground investigation will also need to assess other parameters in addition to the concentration and extent of contamination. In order to estimate and evaluate the risks arising from any contamination, it will be necessary to determine the site geology and hydrogeology and assess the properties of the strata identified, for example bulk density, porosity, hydraulic conductivity, groundwater flow and gas permeability.

It can often be cost-effective to combine geotechnical and contamination investigations, but in so doing the needs and objectives of both must be taken into account. Historically, the objectives of a contamination assessment have often been subordinated to those of the geotechnical investigation and the data obtained on contamination have therefore been of very limited value. One example of the way in which this can happen is when sampling soils from boreholes. A geotechnical engineer may be interested in taking a sample of clay at a depth of, say, five metres in order to establish its load-bearing capacity for piles. However, clay is a very effective barrier against the movement of many contaminants and is therefore unlikely to be contaminated. Testing of the clay for contamination is unlikely to produce much useful information. On many industrial sites contamination is found near the surface, sometimes in made ground. Testing of such material could produce a wealth of information about contamination but very little about the load bearing capacity of the site for piles.

The ground investigation should be designed to provide sufficient information about levels of contaminants to give confidence that the data are representative of the real conditions. The more samples that are taken, the less chance there is that very high concentrations of contaminants or very large areas of contaminated soil would go unnoticed.

There are two principal approaches to designing sampling patterns for a site. These are illustrated schematically in Figure 2.5. They are:

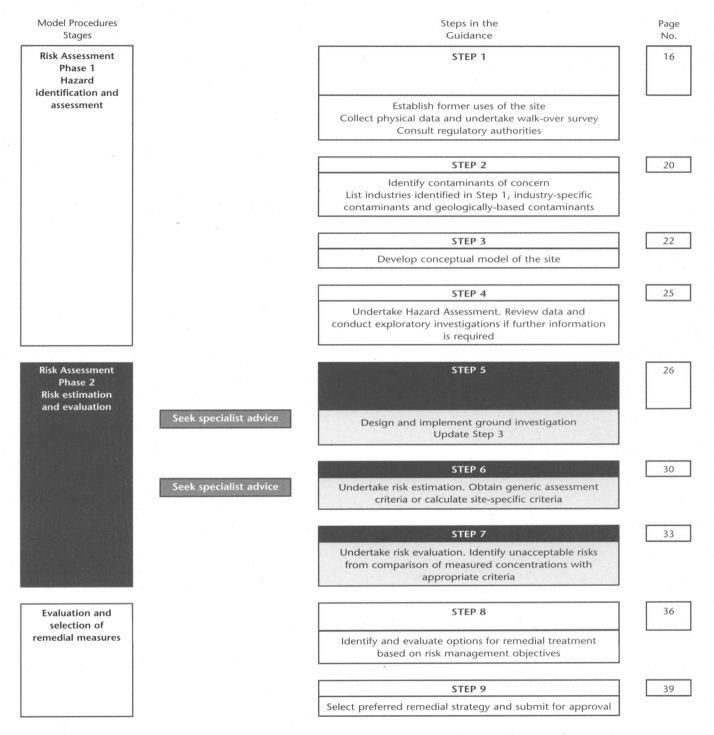

Figure 2.4. Steps in risk assessment phase 2 – risk estimation and evaluation

● targeted, or judgemental, sampling focusing on known, or suspected, point sources or areas of contamination;

● non-targeted or systematic investigation aimed at characterizing the degree of contamination within a defined area or volume of the site.

Targeted sampling recognises that contamination is only rarely distributed evenly across a whole site. Most commonly, it is concentrated in localised areas of the site, or "hot spots". For example, on a former manufacturing site concentrations of contaminants could occur in the following areas:

Step 5 – design and implement ground investigation

- the process area, arising from spillages and leakages over the years;

- the area where process waste was stored or handled prior to shipping off-site;

- fuel storage areas;

- raw materials stores;

- near boilers or power plants.

If plans are available of these areas, or some structures remain, it is sometimes possible to concentrate certain aspects of the investigation on important areas of the site.

Non-targeted investigation is generally based on a systematic sampling regime so that sampling locations are distributed according to a defined pattern. Examples would include a square grid, a herringbone pattern (an offset square grid that offers a more efficient search pattern), or a stratified random pattern (in which the site is divided into a grid and the location of the sampling point within each grid sector is chosen at random). Details of different systematic sampling strategies and the associated probabilities and confidence levels for identifying randomly distributed contamination hot spots of different size and shape are given in the CLR 4 report on sampling strategies.[33] Where little is known about the layout or disposition of former uses, it is normal to ensure that the entire site is covered by the use of a systematic investigation. A sufficient number of sampling positions should be selected to enable an adequate estimate of risks to be made, thus minimising the likelihood of failing to discover a hot spot of a size that could adversely affect the cost and timely completion of the development.

In practice, a combination of judgemental and systematic sampling often offers the best compromise between reliance on a purely statistical approach and using data gathered in earlier steps about the likely location of sources of contamination.

Developers should not underestimate the number of boreholes or trial pits required to obtain a reliable picture of the distribution of contamination on the site. Severely limiting the number of samples may make subsequent steps in the process much more difficult to execute because a higher degree of uncertainty will be introduced. The CLR report on sampling strategies[33] (CLR4) gives an example of the number of sampling positions required to identify a hot spot of a certain size. If it is assumed that a site of 1ha (slightly larger than a football pitch) contains a hot-spot of 100m^2 (1 percent of the site area, or equivalent to half a singles tennis court) then using a herringbone grid pattern, 150 sampling points would be needed to have 95 percent confidence of locating an exploratory hole within the hot spot.

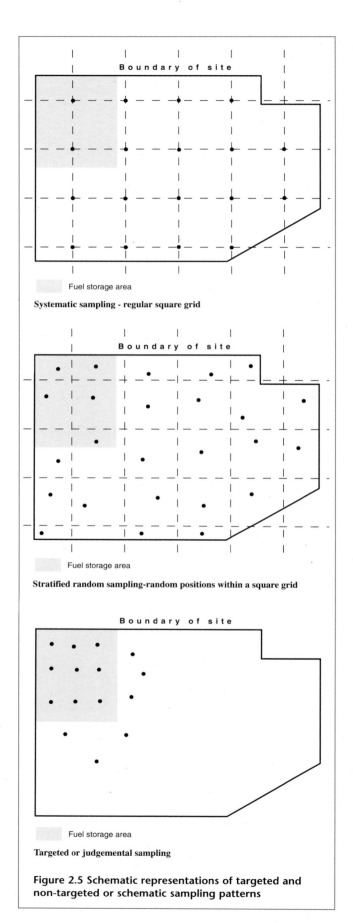

Fuel storage area

Systematic sampling - regular square grid

Fuel storage area

Stratified random sampling-random positions within a square grid

Fuel storage area

Targeted or judgemental sampling

Figure 2.5 Schematic representations of targeted and non-targeted or schematic sampling patterns

Typical densities of sampling grids can vary from 50m to 100m centres for exploratory investigations (see step 4) and from 20m to 25m for detailed investigations.[34] Where contamination is known to be localised, or the presence of highly contaminated hot spots is suspected, sampling grids of 10m centres may be necessary. Sampling at this density may also be appropriate where it is intended to relate the size of grid in the main investigation to the size of garden areas. If this approach is taken, when individual plots are examined to establish whether there are contaminants present, data from at least one sampling position within or close to the boundary of the plot will be available. However, it is unlikely that sampling of an entire site would be required at such a density.

Ground investigations for the purposes of assessing contamination will normally be undertaken using a staged approach. The draft British Standard code of practice[34] which will replace an earlier draft for development[35] indicates that the first stage will require a lower density of sampling than the second and it discusses the spacing of typical densities of sampling grids for both types of investigation. The exploratory investigation described in Step 4 may be adequate as the first stage of a more detailed approach, if designed with that in mind.

The systematic element of a first stage investigation might involve a broad sweep of the site on a defined sampling grid, with samples from various depths being analysed for a broad range of contaminants. The second stage main investigation might be used to look further at any large variations in concentrations of contaminants between adjacent sampling positions. In areas where very high concentrations are measured in the first stage, further samples might be taken. Additional samples might also be taken from "borderline" areas, where concentrations are close to the relevant assessment criteria, any other relevant generic assessment criteria (such as those relating to water quality), or assessment criteria derived on a site-specific basis. In areas of the site where contaminant concentrations fall below the relevant assessment criteria, further samples might be taken for confirmatory purposes, especially where the provisional layout of the site zones these areas for sensitive uses. The basis for multi-stage sampling is therefore to reduce uncertainty and to confirm a sound basis for earlier decisions. Further advice on sampling strategy is provided by the Environment Agency.[36]

2.6.1.3 Investigation techniques

Detailed guidance on site investigations is given in a British Standard code of practice.[37] Various techniques which may be used on contaminated sites are described in the British Standard Code of Practice for Investigation of Potentially Contaminated sites[34].

There are two main types of investigation technique. These are non-intrusive investigations, such as geophysical investigations, and intrusive investigations, which involve trial pits, boreholes or probeholes.

Non-intrusive techniques include the following:

- conductivity and resistivity surveys, which can locate disturbed ground and buried objects and identify variations in groundwater quality;

- magnetic and electromagnetic surveys, which work in a similar way to metal detectors;

- ground penetrating radar, which can identify buried tanks, pipes and voids as well as hydrocarbons;

- seismic techniques, which can identify boundaries between different layers of soil and measure the depth of groundwater;

- surface emissions monitoring using portable gas detection equipment; and

- infra-red thermography, which can detect sources of heat (for example active landfills), and infra-red photography, which can detect stressed vegetation from aerial photographs.

Non-intrusive techniques can be usefully deployed in the first stage of a phased investigation because they can highlight areas for more detailed sampling in the subsequent phase.

Intrusive techniques include the following:

- probing, which typically involves a stainless steel probe with a pointed end which can be pushed or driven just below the surface and can be used to sample for gases or volatile substances in the ground;

- trial pits, excavated using a mechanical digger with a backactor, typically to a depth of about 4m;

- boreholes, which may be constructed to much greater depths than trial pits.

Probing does not allow sampling at significant depth and is therefore often used only for screening. Trial pits are very commonly used because they allow sampling from a range of depths, typically at 0.5m or 1.0m vertical intervals starting at the surface. In the case of housing developments where potential contamination of gardens is an issue, additional samples may be taken from the near surface layers (for example at 0.1m). Trial pits have the advantage that the layers from which the samples are being taken are visible to the site operative, who can take additional samples of any visually suspect material. Boreholes are used to sample at depths beyond that achievable using mechanical excavation. They can also have liners installed and be left in place to allow future monitoring, whereas trial pits are normally backfilled for safety reasons.

Boreholes are most commonly used to sample soils and groundwater at depth and to monitor gas levels in the ground.

2.6.1.4 Analysis

Analysis of samples should be carried out by a laboratory accredited for the appropriate testing methods. Laboratories with UKAS accreditation meet certain quality assurance and quality control requirements for analytical work. However, the UKAS accreditation is obtained for individual analytical methods, and you should check that the certificates relate to the tests required.

Laboratory analytical methods should be selected to provide information relevant to and representative of the site. Detection limits for soil, water, gas and leachability testing should always be specified at concentrations below applicable guideline values and environmental standards. If the methods used have high detection limits, it may be impossible to assess the risk associated with the contaminants on the site, and additional testing may be necessary. The analyst should always be consulted before the analytical programme is decided, to ensure that the information to be provided is relevant and adequate for the purposes of the investigation and is technically and economically acceptable.

2.6.1.5 Uncertainty

No amount of sampling can guarantee to detect all contamination present. Section 3.2.1.2, above, indicates how many sampling positions are required to locate contamination hotspots of a certain size with 95 percent confidence. However, even if the requisite number of samples is taken, there remains a 5 percent chance that contamination will go undetected at the investigation stage. The smaller the hot spot, the more samples will be required to have the same level of confidence that it will be found. Where there are likely to be multiple hot spots even more samples are required to have the same level of confidence of finding them all.

Developers must therefore be aware that even if they commission the most comprehensive ground investigation there is a risk that during development further contamination may be uncovered. If this happens, the conceptual model will need to be amended. This in turn may indicate the need for further investigation, revised risk estimates and a review of the remediation strategy.

Most statistical sampling techniques make important assumptions about the nature of the material sampled and the variation in its properties. Sampling techniques are designed to ensure that a sample is representative of the whole or a known part of the whole, such that analysis of a number of samples allows inferences to be drawn about the properties of the whole based on the properties of the samples. Sampling strategies are relatively easy to design where the material to be sampled is theoretically homogeneous (all the same) or has a

known statistical distribution. However, soil contamination is rarely homogeneous or distributed in a known way. Therefore, the concentration of a contaminant in any location is not necessarily related in any way to its concentration nearby. It is therefore important that the investigation minimises the risks of failure to locate contamination of significant magnitude. This is one important reason why money saved on a site investigation by reducing its scope is often found to be a false economy when major contamination problems are unearthed at a later stage in the development process.

2.6.1.6 Costs

As indicated above, reducing the scope and level of detail of investigations will rarely be cost-effective in the long term, not least because approvals from the planning authority and others may not be forthcoming in the absence of sufficient information on which to assess proposals. The cost of a ground investigation is an important investment which can generate future returns by underpinning the developability of the site. It may provide the evidence that unacceptable risks are unlikely and that remedial actions are not required. If remedial action is necessary, good data can be used to arrive at the optimal layout, which minimises the extent to which remediation will be required, as well as informing the selection of the optimal remediation technologies.

The cost of appropriate investigations will clearly depend on the size of the site, current conditions (for example, breaking through concrete slabs to obtain samples can add to costs), former uses, proposed end use, the environmental setting and the number and type of contaminants to be investigated. As a rough guide, costs of 2-3 percent of the total development cost should be allowed for a comprehensive investigation in accordance with good practice.

STEP 6

2.6.2 – undertake risk estimation

2.6.2.1 Overview

For both new and existing housing developments, it will be essential to estimate and evaluate the long and short-term risks to human health. For new developments, this should include consideration of risks during both the construction phase and post-development. In many cases it may also be necessary to consider risks to the surface water and groundwater environment. Developers would also want to be satisfied that any contaminants in the ground are not likely to damage building materials, services or underground structures. Phytotoxicity (toxicity to plants) is of concern in areas of the development where plants are to be grown, such as gardens and landscaped areas, and some sites may have sensitive ecosystems, such as ponds or woodland, which need to be protected.

Risk estimation can be carried out either by using generic assessment criteria (such as the Guideline Values[26] developed from the CLEA model[27] for assessing the long-term risks to human health) or relevant environmental standards or by deriving site-specific assessment criteria which are tailored to the particular circumstances of the site. The receptors which could be at risk will have been identified in the earlier steps. This step then involves estimating and evaluating all risks which could arise from the contaminants identified. This guidance concentrates mainly on estimating risks to human health, as this will be essential for all housing developments. However, developers should note that other receptors may be equally important on certain sites, and that in some circumstances the risks to other receptors will drive the requirement for remediation. It is likely that specialist advice will be needed for all aspects of risk estimation and evaluation.

The details covered in this step are:

● the use of guideline values for human health as criteria for risk estimation;

● the use of generic criteria or calculated site-specific criteria for human health;

● the use of non-human health criteria; and

● the estimation of risk from short term exposure

2.6.2.2 Risk estimation using guideline values for human health

The Department of the Environment, Transport and the Regions and the Environment Agency are preparing a series of guideline values[26] whose main purpose is to establish whether a site poses actual or potential risks to human health which are unacceptable in the context of the existing or intended use of the site. Guideline values will replace the "trigger concentrations" produced by the Interdepartmental Committee on the Redevelopment of Contaminated Land (ICRCL)[28] in the early 1980s. The guideline values have been derived using the CLEA model,[27] which examines different pathways by which humans can be exposed to soil contaminants and a range of site end uses. A brief description of the CLEA model is given in Appendix 2 and further details are given in CLR 10.[27]
For each contaminant a range of guideline values, rather than a single value, will be available. The range will cover different land uses and, where appropriate, different soil conditions. It is therefore important to select the guideline value appropriate to specific site conditions and the nature of the proposed development. When concentrations of contaminants fall below the appropriate guideline value, individual contaminants or areas of the site can be considered not to pose unacceptable risks to human health and can be eliminated from further consideration. Where concentrations of contaminants exceed the appropriate guideline value, the presumption is that there is sufficient evidence for potentially unacceptable risk to warrant further action. This further action might be

investigation to establish on the basis of more detailed data whether there is an unacceptable risk, or to proceed to the implementation of remedial action.

Different guideline values have been derived for different land uses, including residential developments with and without gardens; parks and open spaces; allotments; and commercial and industrial developments. These reflect the sensitivities and hence the risks associated with the different uses.

Many guideline values are not fixed for each defined land use, but vary according to the concentrations of other substances which can affect their behaviour. For example, soil organic matter affects mercury compounds by binding them so that their potential for mobilisation is reduced. It is therefore important to analyse for soil organic matter when assessing risks from mercury compounds. Soil pH also has an effect on the mobility of many contaminants. Thus, an appropriate guideline value must be derived by taking such factors into account. Factors which affect guideline values are discussed in more detail in CLR 10[27].

In most cases the CLEA guideline values will be appropriate to estimate the long-term risks to human health that may be associated with new or existing housing developments. However, where there is concern about risks to humans already living on a site, for example, because a CLEA guideline value has been exceeded, it may be necessary to establish site-specific assessment criteria. Site-specific criteria may also be required where mixtures of contaminants that could have synergistic effects are identified. Specialist advice will be needed in establishing such criteria.

2.6.2.3 Derivation of site-specific risk assessment criteria for human health from toxicity data and likely exposure

Where guideline values are not yet available or a contaminant has been identified for which a guideline value is not to be developed, it will be necessary either to use other generic criteria or to estimate site specific assessment criteria, based on toxicity data and calculated exposure. A specialist advisor will almost certainly be needed to undertake the work, which should be based upon the comprehensive risk assessment guidance provided in the Model Procedures.[4] An example of the approach to be used is given in Appendix 2. Developers should note that while generic criteria or models developed in other countries, for example the Netherlands or the USA, may be appropriate, it is essential to be certain that the assumptions built into the criteria or models are applicable to the site conditions and to UK policy and good practice.

The regulatory authorities will need to be satisfied with the site-specific criteria proposed and the approach used in its derivation. The specialist advisor should therefore produce a documented assessment which can be evaluated by the regulator, who will be looking for transparency in deriving values, evidence of sound science and clarity in any assumptions made. The Environment Agency is producing further supporting guidance on site-specific assessment of chronic risks to human health from contamination.[65]

2.6.2.4 Non-human health assessment criteria

Risk estimation and evaluation in relation to other potential receptors such as groundwater and surface water, or if relevant, the risks of explosion from methane, generally require specialist advice to be taken. The Model Procedures[4] provide general guidance on carrying out risk estimation for these receptors. Specialist advisors should make reference to the generic criteria or authoritative models available for assessing risks associated with gas, liquids and leachable contaminants within the site, where appropriate.

Assessment concentrations relating to the components of **landfill gas** are given in a Waste Management Paper[38] and Approved Document C in relation to the Building Regulations[22,39]. Approved Document C also considers the types of contaminants that may be left *in situ* beneath building footprints and requires the treatment by removal, filling or sealing of oil and tarry materials, corrosive liquids and combustible materials beneath proposed buildings. Where high levels of contamination are found, removal is often the only viable option. Approved Document C recommends that you seek specialist advice and that the local authority environmental health officer is consulted. Further more detailed guidance on investigation, risk assessment and development of gas affected land has been published by CIRIA and BRE.[62,63,64,69,70,71]

Guidance is provided in CLR1 on estimating and evaluating risks to **groundwater and surface water**.[40] This provides a framework for assessing the impact of contaminated land on groundwater and surface water and a methodology for the derivation of remedial targets for soil and groundwater to protect water resources has been developed on behalf of the Environment Agency. More recent guidance is provided in the Agency's *Policy and Practice for the Protection of Groundwater*[66] and related tools (e.g groundwater vulnerability maps) and the *Methodology for the Derivation of Remedial Targets for Soil and Groundwater to Protect Water Resources*[59]. The Agency has also developed the ConSim model to assist with assessing the risks posed to groundwater by contaminants leaching from soils.[41] Further details of the guidance and models are given in Appendix 2.

The risks to **water quality** are largely related to the mobility or leachability of soil contaminants rather than the total contaminant concentration. The Agency has published guidance on the assessment of contaminant leachability[67], the results of which should be compared with relevant water quality standards. These may be the background water quality, drinking water standards, Environmental Quality Standards (EQS) or others. If leachability test results exceed relevant environmental standards, more detailed assessment of the fate and transport of contaminants in the subsurface may be undertaken using the guidance mentioned above.

In deriving site-specific assessment criteria for pollution of controlled waters, it is important to consider the requirements of EU and UK legislation. In particular, the EC Groundwater Directive (80/68/EEC) requires that List I substances are prevented from entering groundwater, and entry of List II substances is minimised to prevent pollution of groundwater. Similar requirements relating to surface water bodies are made under the EU Dangerous Substances Directive.

Ideally, natural (background) water quality should be protected and land remediated to a standard that ensures this. The environment agencies hold and publish water quality monitoring data that may be used for assessment purposes.

Assessment criteria for risks to **ecological systems** are currently less well developed than those for human health and water quality. Assessment of the risks to aquatic fauna as a result of deterioration in water quality can be made by comparison against Environmental Quality Standards (EQS), but this does not address risks posed by changes or removal of habitat. Consideration needs to be given to the effect of development on protected species (for example badgers, bats and great crested newts), designated areas of nature or ecological importance (such as Sites of Special Scientific Interest, Local Conservation Areas) and the wider environment (such as the protection of trees, hedgerows and other flora and fauna). Advice on these issues may be obtained from English Nature, the Countryside Council for Wales and Scottish National Heritage, or from local nature conservation groups.

2.6.2.5 Estimation of risks from short-term exposure

In some cases there may be risks to human health from short-term exposure to contaminants, for example from direct contact with temporary stockpiles of excavated material or where contaminants at depth have been exposed. Such risks may occur when construction work re-exposes contaminants during development, immediately following completion and occupation of new developments, or several years after completion. Similar risks may occur on existing development where maintenance, repair or refurbishment may involve excavation of the ground.

Table 2.6 gives examples of the ways in which receptors can be exposed to contamination in the short term. The Environment Agency is developing guidance on the subject of short-term risks to human health.[43] Health and Safety Executive guidance[31] is also relevant in dealing with short term risks.

Where risks such as those in Table 2.6 are identified, specialist advice should be sought and an assessment carried out in accordance with the Agency's procedures. Evaluation of these risks should be combined with the evaluation of long-term risks to human health and other receptors to allow a firm conclusion to be drawn about whether there are any unacceptable risks from contamination associated with the site.

STEP 7

2.6.3 – undertake risk evaluation

2.6.3.1 Overview

The purpose of risk evaluation is to establish whether there is a need for risk management action. This involves the collation and review of all information relating to the site in order to:

- address areas of uncertainty and their possible effect on risk estimates;

- identify risks that are considered unacceptable;

- set provisional risk management objectives for addressing the unacceptable risks.

This step includes:

- a commentary on the components of a typical housing development, showing how different components have different sensitivities to contamination and that risks must be considered separately for each;

- procedures for establishing whether risks are considered unacceptable.

2.6.3.2 Components of development

Different components of a residential development, for example homes with gardens or flats with common areas, may have different sensitivities to contamination, based on an assessment of the risks associated with each component. Components of residential development might include:

- the dwelling unit as an entity (taking into account various structural options which may be employed, for example ground bearing slab, suspended floor) where exposure of receptors to certain contaminants is not influenced by associated external areas such as gardens;

- the dwelling unit in combination with:
  - a private garden
  - a communal garden
  - a hard landscaped area;

- a private garden comprising soft landscaping;

- a communal garden/common areas comprising soft landscaping;

- hard landscaping;

Table 2.6   Possible exposure scenarios following completion and occupation of development

Component development	Possible action	Receptors at risk
Gardens associated with residential housing	Penetration of cover material due to excavation, for example extensions/swimming pools/garden features with potential for temporary surface stockpiling and longer-term disposal of materials by spreading at ground level	Occupants of dwelling, for example very young children playing in gardens and occupants in general as consumers of vegetables grown on the property
Communal areas associated with residential housing	Penetration of cover materials due to excavations, for example drainage/services with the potential for temporary surface stockpiling	Children playing in communal areas
Hardstanding areas associated with residential housing	Breaking out for the purposes of ornamental planting	Children playing on communal areas
Drainage	Infiltration of site drainage by contaminated surface water or groundwater	Receiving waters; aquatic ecosystems
Public open space/playing fields	Penetration of cover material due to excavation, for example drainage/services with potential for temporary surface stockpiling	Children playing in the vicinity of stockpiled materials
Allotments	Penetration of cover material due to excavation, for example allotment buildings with potential for temporary surface stockpiling and longer-term disposal of material by spreading at ground level	Users of allotment for example children playing and consumers of vegetables grown on the plot
Hardstandings	Penetration of cover materials due to excavation, for example drainage/services with potential for temporary surface stockpiling of material	Children playing in the vicinity of stockpiled material

Component combination: dwellings, flats (with communal gardens)

Component highways, hardstanding

Component combination: dwellings, houses (with gardens)

Component public open space playing fields

Component combination: dwellings with hardstanding

Figure 2.6 Components of development

- allotments;

- parks/open spaces/playing fields comprising soft landscaping;

- hardstandings and highways, taking into account the range of finishes and forms of construction which are commonly employed;

- services and infrastructure, including water and power supplies, telecoms, drainage and sewerage.

By being aware of the different sensitivities and the nature of the risks associated with each component, developers have the opportunity to optimise the form and layout of development in the context of the risks from contamination at the site, matching the most sensitive components to areas with the lowest risk. Where contamination is significant, remediation costs can be substantially reduced if the development can accommodate alternative, less sensitive components to those originally envisaged. However, where alternative forms of development are proposed, the local planning authority should be consulted on planning issues and constraints.

In addition, the choice of development components can determine the extent to which protection measures can be incorporated. For example, in seeking protection of development from methane and carbon dioxide it is advisable to adopt building forms incorporating ventilated underfloor voids and to avoid sub-surface rooms such as cellars or basements.

Different components of a development may carry different risks, each of which will need to be estimated separately. For example, a detached or semi-detached house with a garden will permit residents to grow vegetables, whereas a block of flats with communal gardens will not normally offer that opportunity. Estimating the risk of exposure to contaminants through consumption of vegetables would therefore be required for the former type of development, but not required for the latter. On the other hand, risks of exposure through skin contact with the ground, for example when playing games, or possible direct ingestion of soil by children would need to be estimated for both types of development.

Figure 2.6 shows some of the different components of development typically found on housing development sites.

2.6.3.3 Identification of unacceptable risks

The risk identification step will have involved the comparison of the perceived and measured levels of concentration of contaminants in the soil derived from the results of site investigations with the relevant generic or site specific assessment criteria.

Risk evaluation involves the collation and review of this information in the context of the proposed development, and its detailed components, in order to identify risks that are considered to be unacceptable. It must involve qualification of the significance of this information with reference to the associated technical uncertainties, and especially the degree of confidence in the accuracy and sufficiency of the data produced, and consideration as to whether the assumptions used in the risk estimation are likely to have over or underestimated the risk.

If the results of the above comparisons are marginal, the assessors may do one of the following:

i)   seek to obtain more data to refine the risk estimates;

ii) judge that the risks are not unacceptable (given any consideration of the limitations of the available data) or;

iii) adopt a precautionary approach which assumes that the risks involved are unacceptable.

Assessors may compare the costs and benefits of the different options available to them. For example, they may find that it is cheaper in the long run to install gas-resistant membranes in all properties in a development where slightly elevated gas concentrations have been found, rather than undertake an extensive methane monitoring programme to produce data which might confirm no exceedance of the relevant criteria. A precautionary approach may also have the benefit of saving time.

Assessors will also take into account the nature of the risk. For example, the existence of phytotoxic metals at concentrations marginally above relevant criteria for ornamental planting might result in some future damage to trees or shrubs. If so, this might be relatively easily corrected by excavation and replacement of a small amount of contaminated soil. The financial and environmental consequences might be quite small and the assessor might decide in such circumstances that the risk is acceptable. In contrast, the existence of methane in the ground at levels only slightly above the relevant criteria would carry a small risk of explosion with damage to property and serious injury or death of the occupants. Such

consequences would be unacceptable and therefore the risk would also be considered unacceptable.

Similarly, where contaminated soil is allowed to remain on a development site it might pose a continuing risk of polluting groundwater, even though the levels of contamination are far below those at which the occupants of the development would be exposed to risk through contact with the soil. In such circumstances, the consequences of groundwater remediation carried out after completion of the development might be considered unacceptable because of the disruption it may cause. The risk might also be deemed unacceptable in view of the developer's potential liability for the groundwater pollution.

2.6.3.4 Development of provisional risk management objectives

When all unacceptable risks have been identified the process of establishing risk management objectives can begin. In general, the risk management objectives will reflect the need to manage the risks associated with each pollutant linkage identified in the conceptual model and subsequently found to be unacceptable. On many sites, a range of objectives may be established in response to the different nature of the risks associated with different pollutant linkages. For example, on a site containing fill material consisting largely of degradable waste material, the risk evaluation may have identified unacceptable risks of the following:

● damage to plants from phytotoxic heavy metals;

● explosion caused by methane ingress into buildings;

● human health effects through direct contact with soil;

● pollution of groundwater by substances leached out of the fill.

In each case the preliminary risk management objectives might be established as:

● prevention of contact between contaminated soil and the root zone in planted areas;

● prevention of contact between contaminated soil and humans in gardens, play areas and public open spaces;

● prevention of methane migration into areas close to buildings;

● reduction of leaching from contaminated soil by preventing water infiltration.

2.7 EVALUATION AND SELECTION OF REMEDIAL MEASURES

The practical steps covering the evaluation and selection of remedial measures are highlighted in Figure 2.7 and discussed in sections 2.7.1 to 2.7.2 of this guidance.

STEP 8

2.7.1 – identify and evaluate options for remedial treatment

2.7.1.1 Overview

The starting point for the development of remedial strategy is the establishment of risk management objectives. In many cases the results of risk evaluation will already have permitted the development of provisional objectives. This step describes the following detailed procedures:

● confirmation of risk management objectives;

● identification and analysis of remedial options.

Guidance on the process of selecting remedial measures is given in the Model Procedures[4] and the CIRIA reports on remedial treatment for contaminated land,[8, 44-54] and in particular Volume V on evaluation and selection of remedial methods.[46] The selection process given in the Model Procedures[4] is briefly summarised below.

Where guideline values or other generic assessment criteria are exceeded for any component of development (see step 7)

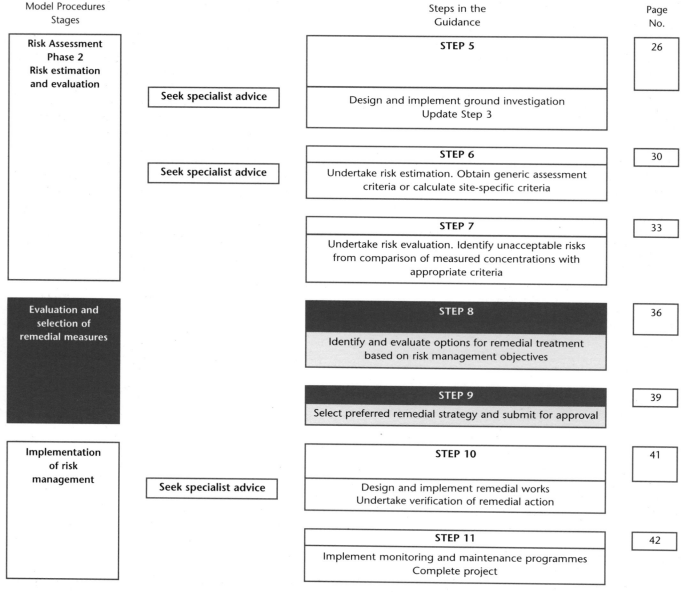

Figure 2.7. Steps in evaluation and selection of remedial pressures

re zoning of the development on site should be assessed as a possible solution. For example, where high levels of contaminants are found in areas designated for sensitive uses, but low levels in areas designated for hardstanding, it may be possible to revise the layout to ensure that the sensitive uses are relocated to areas of low contamination. In this way guideline values for those uses would not be exceeded. Even if revision of layouts cannot accommodate the levels of contaminants found without exceeding guideline values, it may reduce the extent significantly and therefore the cost of remediation required.

The risk estimation and evaluation process will have identified any unacceptable risks from contamination. It is then necessary to decide whether remedial work is required to manage these risks, and, if so, to devise an appropriate remedial strategy.

2.7.1.2 Risk management objectives

Before agreeing a remedial strategy it is important to establish clearly what needs to be achieved by any remediation. This includes not only the preliminary risk-based objectives established in section 2.6.3.4 but also a wider consideration of the circumstances of the land and its management context (see Table 2.7). This statement of what needs to be achieved is termed the remedial objective.

Table 2.7 Examples of the wider circumstances of a site that may need to be taken into account within the remedial objectives

Commercial circumstances	Time, cost, and extent of liabilities.
Legal circumstances	Need to meet certain conditions or to obtain licences/permits.
	Need to manage any civil and criminal liabilities.
Physical circumstances	Location, size, current use, and access to the site.
Engineering circumstances	Need to engineer the ground to ensure safe construction and/or to protect existing buildings.
Other circumstances	Need to ensure suitable amenities/other facilities, for example, provision of suitable gardens as part of an existing or future development.

Conceptually, risk management action will involve breaking the pollutant linkage by use of one or more of the following methods to satisfy the remedial objectives:

- source control: technical action either to remove or in some way modify the source(s) of the contamination. Examples might include excavation and removal, bioremediation or soil venting;

- pathway control: technical action to reduce the ability of the contaminant source to pose a threat to receptors by inhibiting or controlling the pathway. Examples would include the use of engineered cover systems over contaminants left in situ or the use of membranes to prevent gas ingress into buildings;

- receptor control: non-technical actions or controls that alter the likelihood of receptors coming into contact with the contaminants, for example altering the site layout.

A wide range of different techniques can be used individually or in combination to achieve a break in a pollutant linkage.

In determining what needs to be achieved by any remedial strategy you must also consider how it will be accomplished. The statement of any remedial objective should take account of any changes resulting from the selected approach and technique(s), such as:

- how will the remedial objective be measured? For example, the outcome of an ex situ bioremediation scheme may be a measured reduction in the concentration of the contamination in the soil heap. However, for a cover system, the properties of the liner in terms of its thickness and engineered properties are more appropriate than measuring contaminant concentration beneath it.

- where is the remedial objective to be measured? This would take into account, for example, the media type, location of samples, and extent of area/volume to be covered.

The remedial objectives must take this into account to an increasing level of detail, as the most appropriate remedial strategy becomes clearer. The remedial objectives should therefore, be kept under review and revised accordingly throughout the evaluation, selection, and implementation process outlined in steps 9 and 10.

When the remedial objectives have been defined it will be necessary to confirm that all the appropriate information is available, particularly in relation to pollutant linkages and the associated risks, to proceed with the selection of remedial measures.

2.7.1.3 Identification and analysis of remedial options

Having identified the preliminary remedial objectives, the next step is to devise a shortlist of potentially suitable remedial options. They may involve applying a single technique or a combination of methods to deal with different contaminants, risks, and site circumstances. The shortlisted options should be identified on the basis of:

- provisional effectiveness in dealing with the contaminants of concern;

- provisional consideration of the wider circumstances of the site (see Table 2.7).

The short listing should take account of the available information and any associated uncertainties. For example, a technique may be initially identified as potentially suitable on the basis of its general effectiveness, but later, more site-specific evaluation may eventually lead to it being discounted.

A short list may be drawn up of options appropriate for treating parts or all of the site. The options may include both technical measures, for example bioremediation or soil venting, and non-technical measures, such as altering the site layout.

The short listed options are then subject to detailed analysis to consider the advantages and disadvantages of each approach. It will include:

- discounting of one or more options on the basis of detailed consideration of site-specific effectiveness and the wider circumstances of the site. For example, a treatability or pilot-scale evaluation may demonstrate that an initially promising approach is unlikely to be effective.

- balancing of a range of issues to identify the preferred solution. This should take account of the wider circumstances of the site and any specific requirements of the remedial objectives.

The analysis should be as comprehensive as possible, necessitating the collection of additional information as appropriate. The range of issues to be considered include (not in any particular order):

- costs and benefits (including finance considerations and liability);

- effectiveness of meeting remedial objectives (including site-specific, timeliness, durability, risk-based and non risk-based objectives);

- wider environmental effects (including disruption to amenity, sustainability, and the requirement to meet certain conditions or obtain a licence or permit);

- practical operational issues (for example, site access, availability of services, agreed access);

- aftercare issues (for example, the need to maintain and inspect remedial systems or to establish longer term groundwater monitoring).

This assessment may be carried out on a simple qualitative basis or may involve more detailed semi-quantitative assessment. In either case, it is advisable that some prioritisation or weighting is applied to these different factors, so that the most relevant, balanced assessment can be made. It may be worth investing more time and resources in this

selection process where the choices to be made are particularly difficult, for example if a wide range of different stakeholders is involved. However, it is very important that the process is carefully documented with a high degree of clarity and transparency, to enable the selection of the final strategy to be explained to the different stakeholders (such as the general public, the company shareholders, the planning authority, and/or the Environment Agency).

Further information on this selection process can be found in the Model Procedures.[4]

An increasing number of remedial treatment methods is available commercially in the UK. In order to arrive at the optimum strategy in terms of its ability to meet the risk management objectives as well as accommodate management or cost constraints, careful consideration of the applications and reliability of each is required.

The options available for remedial treatment fall into two categories, namely technical options, involving direct action on the contaminants or their behaviour, and non-technical options, which involve management of the receptor behaviour to alter its ability to come into contact with contaminants. Technical options include:

- civil engineering approaches, for example containment using cover systems, containment using in-ground barriers, and excavation and disposal;

- biological based approaches, for example bioventing; in situ bioremediation; landfarming; and windrow turning;

- managed natural attenuation,[66] when extended time scales are available for remediation;

- chemical based approaches, for example reactive walls, soil flushing, and solvent extraction;

- physical based approaches, for example dual phase vacuum extraction, air sparging; physico-chemical washing, soil vapour extraction; and soil washing;

- solidification and stabilisation based approaches, for example cement and pozzolan systems, lime based systems, and vitrification;

- thermal based approaches, for example incineration, and thermal desorption.

Non-technical options might include the following:

- changing the land use;

- changing the site layout;

- controls over behaviour of receptor/site use (for example through the use of planning conditions and restrictive covenants).

Sometimes the design of a site for housing can meet some of the risk management objectives in itself. For example, blocks of flats with extensive hard cover for roads and parking areas with minimal planting and no private gardens can create an effective barrier between occupants of the flats and contaminated soil lying beneath the hard standing and prevent continued leaching of contaminants into groundwater. Some design elements of housing can pose particular problems, however, where contaminants are present. In such circumstances specialist advice may be required. The relevant design elements are shown in Table 2.8. Particular care should be taken to ensure that geotechnical solutions for poor ground conditions do not conflict with proposed remedial treatment for contamination.

Descriptions of an extensive range of remediation technologies, including chemical, physical and biological treatment methods, and their applicability are in preparation. The most applicable of these are summarised in Appendix 6 of this guidance. Individual technologies are listed in Appendix 7. All of those listed are commercially available in the UK, although some have a limited track record. For each technology, details of the following are provided:

- technology description;

- contaminants that can be treated by the technology;

- media that can be treated (for example soil types, groundwater);

- treatment costs;

- treatment timescales;

- technical limitations.

If contamination which has not been identified in the earlier steps is revealed during the course of site development or remediation, it will be necessary to re-evaluate the risks and perhaps adopt a revised remedial strategy. This will have to include consideration of the risks associated with the areas of the site which have already been developed. In such a case, appropriate in situ remedial options that can be used without disturbing the existing development may be deemed more appropriate. Specialist advice should be sought in such situations.

STEP 9
2.7.2 – select preferred remedial strategy
2.7.2.1 Overview

From the detailed analysis of short listed remedial options, a preferred remedial strategy can be established. This is achieved by identifying the strategy which will best meet remedial objectives through assessing comparative effectiveness of the identified options against the various prioritised criteria identified in the previous analytical process.

The results of the decision making process should be well documented, to enable regulators and other interested parties to understand the various considerations and priorities which have informed the process, and to facilitate their acceptance of the strategy.

Where site conditions are complex and there are many different conflicting technical and non-technical priorities to

Table 2.8 Future development design options needing specialist advice

Design option	Commentary
Buildings design:	
Piled foundations	May create preferential flow paths for contaminant through otherwise protective cover layers overlying aquifers.
Specialist 'vibro' foundations	Incorporation of granular material as part of the technique may create preferential flow paths for contaminants to underlying layers. Similarly, preferential flow paths for volatile contaminants may be formed under dwellings.
	Where limestone is used, acidity (low pH) in the soil may cause it to decompose to produce carbon dioxide.
Drainage:	
Soakaways	As with vibro compaction techniques (above), preferential flow paths may be created. Contaminants in the soil may be mobilised by water flowing through it.
'Open ditch' drainage systems	May create increased potential for unnecessary exposure of sensitive receptors for example humans to contaminants remaining on site.
Surface water features, such as ponds	As for open ditches (above).
Storm water balancing ponds	As for open ditches (above).

consider, specialist advice can be sought to assist in the whole process of developing of the remediation strategy

2.7.2.2 Documentation and approvals

The process of remediation itself may be subject to a number of regulatory controls requiring permission to proceed with works. These are, in addition to any planning consent and approvals under the Building Regulations, CDM Regulations, and other occupational health and safety legislation. These include:

● waste management licensing under Part II of EPA 1990 (including registered exemptions, site licences, mobile plant licences, and Environment Agency enforcement positions);

● authorisations under Part I of EPA 1990;

● authorisations under the Groundwater Regulations 1998;

● consents under the Water Resources Act 1991 and the Water Industry Act 1991;

● abstraction licences under the Water Resources Act 1991.

If there is any doubt over whether an appropriate authorisation, licence or consent is or is not required then specialist advice should be sought before any works are agreed and implemented.

Documentation to be submitted to the authorities at this point should in general include a report of the ground investigation, risk assessment and remedial strategy, consisting of:

● purpose and aims of the report;

● summary of available site information;

● ground investigation methodology;

● works completed;

● results/findings of work relating to geology, hydrogeology and soil contamination;

assessment of hazards;

● estimation and evaluation of risks;

● evaluation of remedial options;

● the preferred remedial strategy.

Reports should be clear, transparent and based on sound science. A checklist of typical reports produced for a housing development is provided in Appendix 3.

At this stage it may also be appropriate to seek community acceptance of the proposals, especially where remedial works are likely to be highly visible and result in a certain amount of disruption.

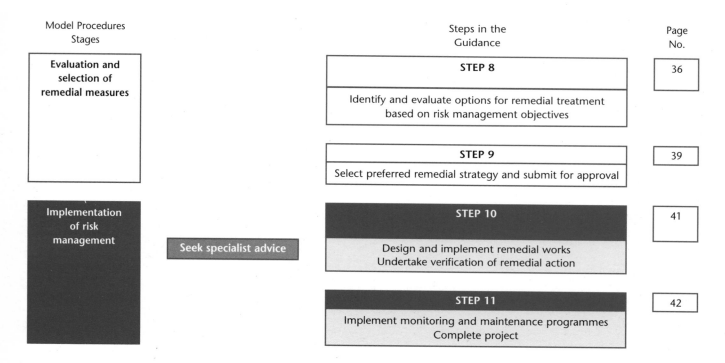

Figure 2.8   Steps in implementation of risk management actions

2.8 IMPLEMENTATION OF RISK MANAGEMENT OPTIONS

Risk management is implemented through submission of plans for approval, design and construction of the remedial works, and monitoring and validation of the activities during construction and after completion of the works. These activities are summarised in Figure 2.8 and described in sections 2.8.1 and 2.8.2 of this guidance.

STEP 10

2.8.1 – design and implement remedial works

2.8.1.1 Overview

By the end of step 9 a remedial strategy will have been determined. In this step, the design and procurement of the remedial works are carried out. Since this step often represents the first stage of development work on site it is appropriate to ensure that all formal approvals necessary for the development and remedial work to proceed have been identified. In addition, the appropriate documents required to support applications for approval should have been prepared (see step 9).

This step includes details of the following activities:

- development of an implementation plan;
- implementation of remedial works;
- verification of remedial works.

2.8.1.2 Development of an implementation plan

The principal tasks are to design and specify the remedial works required and to formulate an implementation plan. In developing the implementation of risk management action the procedures set out the Model Procedures[4] should be followed. The key steps are as follows:

- confirm that the objectives remain relevant for detailed design;
- determine what constitutes completion of the remedial treatment (see below);
- identify the detailed design factors and ensure adequate data are available;
- design and specify the remedial treatment;
- prepare an implementation plan;
- procure the remedial treatment.

Guidance on the design and specification of remedial measures is given in the CIRIA reports *Remedial Treatment for Contaminated Land*, in particular volumes V to IX[47-51].

The implementation plan will document all the data required in order to be able to implement the risk management action

effectively and efficiently. The starting point for this is the selection of the remedial strategy. At this stage, however, detailed design issues may be identified at this stage that require further information to enable detailed design and completion of the implementation plan prior to procurement of the remedial works.

Sufficient data will also be required to enable appropriate procurement. The level of information needed will reflect the preferred procurement route. For example, procurement of contracting services against a detailed design prepared by the design advisor will require detailed specification, drawings and bills of quantities. Alternative procurement could be via a design and implement route where a performance specification would be issued and a detailed method statement and schedule of costs prepared by the contractor. Preferences for procurement arrangements should be established prior to developing any detailed work on design.

Aspects to consider when formulating the implementation plan include the following:

- client and legal issues, including
  - project management
  - programme
  - specifications and contract documentation
  - warranties, procurement route and conditions of contract
  - resources, roles and responsibilities including lines of communication
  - third party approvals
  - health and safety requirements
  - quality management systems;

- technical issues, including
  - scope of work
  - remedial objectives
  - site preparation and operational requirements
  - site supervision
  - monitoring requirements
  - verification requirements
  - post treatment management
  - contingency planning
  - systems required for documenting and reporting remedial action including variations during the remedial treatment;

- financial issues, including
  - capital costs of works
  - running costs
  - disposal costs
  - supervision costs
  - monitoring and verification costs
  - professional fees
  - contingencies
  - insurance premiums
  - grant funding.

2.8.1.3 Implementation

The health and safety file should be updated before work on implementation commences. A suitably experienced person should supervise the implementation of remedial measures. Clear records of site works should be maintained to allow "as built" records to be produced on completion. The appropriate regulatory authorities should be kept informed of progress and in particular any variations from the proposed remedial strategy. This is best achieved by the preparation of progress reports conforming to the guidance given in the Model Procedures.[4]

During and after completion of this step it is important to document departures from the original remedial strategy as a result of new findings on contamination of the land. Documentation of work undertaken will be developed from site notes, diaries and progress reporting. In the context of this guidance such a document should address the following:

- contaminant concentrations and locations where contaminants are left in-situ;

- extent and magnitude of any groundwater contamination;

- records of physical characteristics and contamination status of materials which have been redistributed on site;

- records of materials disposed of off-site;

- records of physical characteristics and contamination status of any imported materials;

- monitoring and maintenance requirements.

2.8.1.4 Verification

The completed works should be verified against the original risk management objectives of the remedial strategy. Verification may also be required where there is a requirement for:

- monitoring to meet licence/permit conditions;

- monitoring of risks caused by activities on-site during the works;

- ongoing validation testing during the works to prove that the remedial objectives are being met.

Examples of verification activities undertaken to meet these requirements include:

- measuring the quality and quantity of a discharge to a watercourse during dewatering of excavations to confirm compliance with discharge consents;

- chemical testing of potentially contaminated material revealed during development, to confirm that risk estimates and risk evaluation are still valid;

- confirmatory chemical testing of imported fill to confirm that it complies with any specification;

- testing of groundwater samples to check that treatment has achieved the desired reduction in levels of contamination and continues to achieve these reductions;

- monitoring of soil vapour concentrations of volatile contaminants during and immediately after completion of remediation involving soil vapour or vacuum extraction or air sparging to check that levels have been reduced in accordance with the objectives;

- monitoring of gas concentrations in underfloor voids to check that ventilation systems or barriers are working;

- inspection of works to check that they are built in accordance with the specification.

The latter activity is a routine task on all construction sites. Checking procedures should, however, ensure that the works are not only in accordance with the development design requirements but also meet risk management objectives. The whole process must be well documented and available for inspection throughout the contract period, and retained.

Progress reports will enable these and other aspects (for example progress against programme, or expenditure against budget) to be monitored. They will also assist assessment of the significance of any variations against the implementation plan, including any need to modify the planned works (for example to reflect the actual extent of contamination identified and consequential revisions to risk estimates).

STEP 11

2.8.2 – implement monitoring and maintenance programmes and complete project

2.8.2.1 Overview

This step commences at about the time that the development is complete. The purpose of long-term monitoring is to ensure that remedial treatment continues to be effective during the post-completion phase. A long-term maintenance plan may also be developed to ensure that remedial works remain in good repair.

This step covers:

- the circumstances in which long term monitoring and maintenance might be required;

- development of a monitoring and maintenance plan;

- completion of the development project.

2.8.2.2 Long term monitoring and maintenance requirements

If all significant contaminants are removed or destroyed at the end of step 10 and verification shows that the remedial objectives have been met, no further action is needed apart from ensuring that comprehensive, appropriate documentation is prepared and maintained. If, however, contaminants remain or the end-point of remedial treatment is uncertain, post-treatment management, comprising monitoring and/or maintenance will be required. Sometimes, long term monitoring may be made a condition of a planning permission or waste management licence.

Post-completion monitoring may be required for a period ranging from a few weeks or months up to several years. For example, where a groundwater remediation scheme has been implemented, monitoring to check on groundwater quality and to ensure that contamination levels do not begin to rise again might be required over a six-month period (unless the levels are observed to change, in which case it might be extended). In contrast, landfill gas monitoring might be carried out over a period of several years.

Requirements for on going monitoring and maintenance may have been identified as follows:

- where the need has been identified and planned, and is set out in the implementation plan;

- where the remedial works have been undertaken and the implementation plan has been subject to variation, indicating the need for monitoring or maintenance;

- as part of an option to monitor arising from decisions on completion of risk evaluation, where the identified risks do not warrant specific remedial action.

2.8.2.3 Development of a monitoring and maintenance plan

Where the need for ongoing monitoring and maintenance has not been set out in an implementation plan, a separate plan for undertaking the monitoring and maintenance is required. This should set out the scope and content of monitoring and maintenance, and arrangements for reporting on and responding to the findings of the programme.

Aspects to be considered in developing a monitoring and maintenance plan include:

- objectives;

- detailed specification of work required;

- resources and responsibilities for carrying out the work;

- location and details of monitoring points (existing and/or new points required);

- frequency and duration of monitoring;

- substances to be tested and analytical procedures to be used including limits of detection;

- equipment to be used, including calibration requirements;

- requirements for record keeping and reporting;

- criteria for evaluating the findings;

- options for actions and responsibility for decisions if criteria are not met;

- regulatory approvals.

The monitoring plan needs to set out response actions in the event that monitoring results do not meet the previously determined acceptance criteria. The response actions could form part of the contingency planning considered as part of the detailed design factors for the project. Depending on the circumstances of the project, actions could be to:

- verify that the measurement has been correctly recorded;

- consider ancillary data;

- increase the number of monitoring locations;

- determine the actual extent of the problem;

- increase the frequency of monitoring, possibly to continuous monitoring with alarms;

- reassess the risk in light of the data now available on the site;

- modify the existing remedial works;

- consider alternative remedial methods.

Monitoring reports should include monitoring objectives, details of site visits and analytical data collected, interpretation of results, assessment of compliance and requirements for and frequency of further monitoring and maintenance. Supporting information should include sampling and analytical procedures used, type of equipment used, details of monitoring points used, and location plan of monitoring points.

2.8.2.4 Project completion

Project "completion" needs to be established on a case by case basis, and in particular will reflect the risk management strategy being implemented and the circumstances in which the work is being carried out. Examples include:

- a scheme involving only remedial works where completion involves meeting pre-determined remedial standards;

- a scheme involving remedial works as part of a development scheme where completion may have been defined under the conditions of contract as issue of the final certificate;

- a scheme involving remedial works either in isolation or as part of a development scheme where the scheme is undertaken in a number of discrete phases and completion is measured against an individual phase;

- a remedial scheme where ongoing environmental monitoring is needed after the remedial works have been implemented and completion is based on the monitoring meeting pre-determined criteria;

- a remedial scheme where there is a set maintenance period after pre determined remedial standards have been met and completion occurs when the maintenance period ends;

- a remedial scheme that has been implemented against pre determined remedial standards but completion is measured against a risk management strategy and/or completion report, being formally accepted by regulatory authorities (for example through correspondence with the relevant environment agency or discharge of appropriate planning conditions).

REFERENCES

1. Department of the Environment, Transport and the Regions (2000) *Revision of Planning Policy Guidance Note No. 3: Housing*, London: HMSO.

2. Department of the Environment, Transport and the Regions (1999) First provisional results from phase 1 of the National Land Use Database. DETR Statistical Bulletin.

3. Government of Great Britain (1990) *Environmental Protection Act 1990: Part IIA Contaminated Land* (inserted by the Environment Act 1995).

4. Department of the Environment, Transport and the Regions and Environment Agency (2000) *Model Procedures for the Management of Contaminated Land. Contaminated Land Research Report No. 11*, London: Department of the Environment, Transport and the Regions, in press.

5. Department of the Environment, Transport and the Regions (February 2000) *Draft DETR Circular. Environmental Protection Act 1990: Part IIA Contaminated Land*. London: Department of the Environment.

6. NATO/CCMS (1989) *The NATO/CCMS Pilot Study on Demonstration of Remedial Action Technologies for Contaminated Land and Groundwater*. Warren Spring Laboratory WSL Report WR 817.

7. Department of the Environment and Welsh Office (1994) *Paying for Our Past*. Consultation paper.

8. Harris, M.R. Herbert S.M. and Smith, M.A. (1995) *Remedial Treatment for Contaminated Land*. Volume I: Introduction and guide, Special Publication 101, London: Construction Industry Research and Information Association (CIRIA).

9. Building Research Establishment (1991) *Sulphate and Acid Resistance of Concrete in the Ground*, Digest 363, Watford: Building Research Establishment.

10. Raybould, J.G. Rowan, S.P. and Barry, D.L. (1995) *Methane Investigation Strategies*, Report 150. London: CIRIA.

11. Building Research Establishment (1999) *Radon: Guidance on Protective Measures for New Dwellings*, Report BR 211, 3rd edition, Watford: Building Research Establishment.

12. Urban Task Force (1999) *Towards An Urban Renaissance*. Report of the Urban Task Force chaired by Lord Rogers of Riverside. London: SPON.

13. Department of the Environment (various dates) *Industry Profiles*. 48 Volumes, Garston: Building Research Establishment.

14. Department of the Environment (1994) *Framework for Contaminated Land*. Outcome of the Government's review and conclusions from the consultation paper *Paying for our Past*. London: Department of the Environment and Welsh Office.

15. Department of the Environment, Transport and the Regions (1999) *The Key to Easier Home Buying and Selling*. Task Group Report. London: Department of the Environment, Transport and the Regions.

16. Scotland and Northern Ireland Forum for Environmental Research (1999) *Communicating Understanding of Contaminated Land Risks*. SNIFFER Project Number SR97(11)F.

17. Department of the Environment (1997) *Quality Assurance in Environmental Consultancy*. Contaminated Land Research Report No. 12, London: Department of the Environment.

18. Government of Great Britain (1995) *Town and Country Planning (General Permitted Development) Order*.

19. Government of Great Britain (1990) *Town and Country Planning Act*.

20. Government of Great Britain (1974) *Heath and Safety at Work Act*.

21. Government of Great Britain (1994) *Construction Design and Management Regulations*.

22. Government of Great Britain (1991) *Building Regulations*.

23. NHBC (1999) *NHBC Standards*. Chapter 4.1, "Land quality - managing ground conditions".

24. Government of Great Britain (1994) *Waste Management Licensing Regulations*.

25. Environment Agency (1997) *Interim Guidance on the Disposal of "Contaminated Soils"*. Guidance note.

26. Department of the Environment, Transport and the Regions and Environment Agency (2000) *Guideline Values for Contamination in Soils*. Contaminated Land Research Report GV series, London: Department of the Environment, Transport and the Regions, in press.

27. Department of the Environment, Transport and the Regions (2000) *The Contaminated Land Exposure Assessment Model (CLEA): Technical Basis and Algorithms*. Contaminated Land Research Report No. 10, London: Department of the Environment, Transport and the Regions, in press.

28. Interdepartmental Committeee on the Reclamation of Contaminated Land (1987) *Guidance on the Assessment and Redevelopment of Contaminated Land*. ICRCL 59/83, 2nd ed.

29. Department of the Environment (1994) *Documentary Research on Industrial Sites.* Contaminated Land Research Report No. 3, London: Department of the Environment.

30. Department of the Environment (1994) *Guidance on Preliminary Site Inspection of Contaminated Land.* Contaminated Land Research Report No. 2 London: Department of the Environment.

31. Health and Safety Executive (1991) *Protection of Workers and the General Public during the Development of Contaminated Land,* London: HMSO.

32. J.E. Steeds, E. Shepherd and D.L. Barry. (1996) *A Guide for Safe Working Practices on Contaminated Sites.* CIRIA Report No. 132, London: CIRIA.

33. Department of the Environment (1994) *Sampling Strategies for Contaminated Land.* Contaminated Land Research Report No. 4, London: Department of the Environment.

34. British Standards Institution (2000) *Code of Practice for Investigation of Potentially Contaminated Sites* (in preparation).

35. British Standards Institution (1988) *Code of Practice for the Identification of Potentially Contaminated Land and its Investigation.* Draft for Development DD175, London: British Standards Institution.

36. Environment Agency (1999) *Development of Soil Sampling Strategies for Contaminated Land,* Bristol: Environment Agency (in preparation).

37. British Standards Institution (1981) BS5930: *Code of Practice for Site Investigation,* London: British Standards Institution.

38. Department of the Environment (1991) *Landfill Gas, Waste Management Paper 27,* 2nd edition, London: HMSO.

39. Department of the Environment & Welsh Office (1991) *Site Preparation and Resistance to Moisture. The Building Regulations Approved Document C,* London: HMSO.

40. Department of the Environment (1994) *A Framework for Assessing the Impact of Contaminated Land on Groundwater and Surface Water.* Contaminated Land Research Report No. 1, London: Department of the Environment.

41. Environment Agency (1999) *ConSim Contamination Impact on Groundwater: Simulation by Monte Carlo Method.* (prepared by Golder Associates UK Ltd.) Bristol: Environment Agency.

42. European Economic Community (1996) *Directive on Pollution Caused by Certain Dangerous Substances Discharged into the Aquatic Environment of the Community.* 76/464/EEC.

43. Environment Agency (2000) *Assessing the Possible Short term Risks to Health and the Environment of Contaminated Land.* Bristol: Environment Agency (in preparation).

44. Harris, M.R., Herbert, S.M., and Smith, M.A. (1995) *Remedial Treatment for Contaminated Land.* Volume II: "Decommissioning, decontamination and demolition" special publication 102, London: CIRIA.

45. Harris, M.R., Herbert, S.M., and Smith, M.A. (1995) *Remedial Treatment for Contaminated Land.* Volume III: "Site investigation and assessment", special publication 103, London: CIRIA.

46. Harris, M.R., Herbert, S.M., and Smith, M.A. (1995) *Remedial Treatment for Contaminated Land.* Volume IV: "Classification and selection of remedial methods", special publication 104, London: CIRIA.

47. Harris, M.R., Herbert, S.M., and Smith, M.A. (1995) *Remedial Treatment for Contaminated Land.* Volume V: "Excavation and disposal," special publication 105, London: CIRIA.

48. Harris, M.R., Herbert, S.M., and Smith, M.A. (1995) *Remedial Treatment for Contaminated Land.* Volume VI: "Containment and hydraulic measures," special publication 106, London: CIRIA.

49. Harris, M.R., Herbert, S.M., and Smith, M.A. (1995) *Remedial Treatment for Contaminated Land.* Volume VII: "Ex-situ remedial methods for soils, sludges and sediments," special publication 107, London: CIRIA.

50. Harris, M.R., Herbert, S.M., and Smith, M.A. (1995) *Remedial Treatment for Contaminated Land.* Volume VIII: "Ex-situ remedial methods for contaminated groundwater and other liquids", special publication 108, London: CIRIA.

51. Harris, M.R., Herbert, S.M., and Smith, M.A. *Remedial Treatment for Contaminated Land.* Volume IX: "In-situ methods of remediation", special publication 109, CIRIA (London) (1995).

52. Harris, M.R., Herbert, S.M., and Smith, M.A. (1995) *Remedial Treatment for Contaminated Land.* Vol X : "Special situations", special publication 110, London: CIRIA.

53. Harris, M.R., Herbert, S.M., and Smith, M.A. (1995) *Remedial Treatment for Contaminated Land.* Vol XI : "Planning and management", special publication 111, London: CIRIA.

54. Harris, M.R., Herbert, S.M., and Smith, M.A. (1998) *Remedial Treatment for Contaminated Land.* Volume XII: "Policy and legislation", special publication 112, London: CIRIA.

55. Environment Agency (1999) *Mobile Plant Licences (Remedial Treatment of Contaminated Soils): Working Plan Guidance and Library of Licence Conditions.* Draft guidance.

56. Department of the Environment, Transport and the Regions (2000) *Potential Contaminants for the Assessment of Land.*

Contaminated Land Research Report, London: Department of the Environment, Transport and the Regions, in press

57. Department of the Environment (1995) *Prioritisation and Categorisation Procedure for Sites which may be Contaminated.* Contaminated Land Research Report No. 6, London: Department of the Environment.

58. Department of the Environment, Transport and the Regions and Environment Agency (2000) *Contaminants in Soils: Collation of Toxicological Data and Intake Values for Humans.* Contaminated Land Research Report No. 9, London: Department of the Environment, Transport and the Regions, in press.

59. Environment Agency (1999) *Methodology for the Derivation of Remedial Targets for Soil and Groundwater to Protect Water Resources,* R&D publication 20. Bristol: Environment Agency.

60. American Society for Testing and Materials (1995) *Risk-based Corrective Action Applied at Petroleum Release Sites.* Standard guide, E1739-95.

61. Construction Industry Research and Information Association (1996) *Remedial Treatment of Contaminated Land Using In-ground Barriers Liners and Covers,* Special Publication 124, London: CIRIA.

62. Construction Industry Research and Information Association Card, B. (1995) *Protecting Development from Methane,* Report 149, London: (CIRIA).

63. Building Research Establishment (1991) *Construction of new buildings on gas contaminated land* Report BR 212, Watford: Building Research Establishment.

64. Department of the Environment (1994) *Householders' Guide to Radon.* London: HMSO.

65. Environment Agency (2000) *Guidance on Site Specific Assessment of Chronic Risks to Human Health from Contamination;* R & D Project P5-041, Bristol, Environment Agency (in preparation).

66. Environment Agency (1998) *Policy and Practice for the Protection of Groundwater (2nd Edition),* London The Stationary Office.

67. National Rivers Authority (1994) *Leaching Tests for the Assessment of Contaminated Land:* Interim NRA Guidance, NRA R&D Note 301, Bristol, Environment Agency.

68. Environment Agency (2000) *Methodology for the Comparison of the CLEA Model with other human health risk assessment packages,* Project NC/06/07 (in preparation).

69. Harries, C.R. Witherington, P.J. and McEntree, J.M. (1995) *Interpreting measurements of gas in the ground* Report 151, London: CIRIA

70. O'Riordan, N.J. and Milloy, C.J. (1995) *Risk Assessment for methane and other gases in the ground.* Report 152, London:CIRIA

71. Building Research Establishment, (2000) *Protection of Housing from Gas Contaminated Land,* Watford, BRE.

Appendices

APPENDIX 1. Key contaminants associated with industrial uses of land

Comprehensive lists of contaminants associated with industrial uses of land appear in each of the Department of the Environment Industry Profiles. The number of contaminants associated with industrial uses varies, with some profiles listing over 100 different substances. The most significant contaminants associated with each, selected on the basis of frequency of occurrence, existence of information on hazards and availability of analytical methods are listed in Tables A1.1 (metals, semi-metals and inorganic chemicals) and A1.2 (organic chemicals). The tables are taken from the DETR CLR report on contaminants for the assessment of land[56].

Table A1.1. Metals, semi-metals and inorganic chemicals associated with industrial uses of land

Industry	As	Ba	Be	Cd	Cr	Cu	Pb	Hg	Ni	Se	V	Zn	CN–free	CN–complex	NO3–	SO4²⁻	S²⁻	Asbestos	B	pH	S0
Airports	✓					✓								✓						✓	
Animal and animal products processing works				✓	✓												✓			✓	
Asbestos manufacturing works				✓	✓													✓			
Ceramics, cement and asphalt manufacturing works	✓			✓	✓	✓	✓		✓			✓				✓	✓	✓		✓	
Charcoal works	✓			✓	✓	✓	✓	✓		✓		✓	✓		✓	✓				✓	✓
Chemical works: coatings and printing inks manufacturing works		✓			✓	✓	✓	✓	✓			✓								✓	✓
Chemical works: cosmetics and toiletries manufacturing works						✓						✓					✓			✓	
Chemical works: disinfectants manufacturing works		✓				✓	✓	✓	✓			✓				✓				✓	
Chemical works: explosives, propellants and pyrotechnics manufacturing works	✓	✓			✓	✓	✓		✓			✓	✓		✓	✓		✓	✓	✓	
Chemical works: fertiliser manufacturing works	✓			✓	✓	✓	✓	✓	✓			✓			✓	✓		✓		✓	
Chemical works: fine chemicals manufacturing works	✓			✓	✓	✓	✓	✓			✓	✓			✓	✓	✓	✓		✓	
Chemical works: inorganic chemicals manufacturing works	✓	✓		✓	✓	✓	✓	✓		✓	✓	✓	✓		✓	✓		✓	✓	✓	
Chemical works: linoleum vinyl and bitumen-based floor covering manufacturing works	✓			✓		✓	✓														
Chemical works: mastics, sealants, adhesives and roofing felt manufacturing works	✓	✓			✓	✓	✓	✓				✓				✓		✓		✓	
Chemical works: organic chemicals manufacturing works	✓			✓	✓	✓	✓		✓		✓		✓			✓		✓		✓	
Chemical works: pesticides manufacturing works	✓			✓	✓	✓	✓	✓	✓		✓	✓			✓	✓		✓	✓	✓	
Chemical works: pharmaceuticals manufacturing works	✓				✓	✓	✓	✓	✓	✓	✓		✓	✓	✓	✓	✓	✓			✓
Chemical works: rubber processing works (including works manufacturing tyres and other rubber products)							✓					✓					✓	✓	✓		✓
Chemical works: soap and detergent manufacturing works					✓	✓	✓													✓	
Dockyards and dockland	✓			✓	✓	✓	✓	✓	✓			✓	✓			✓	✓	✓		✓	
Dry cleaners	✓			✓	✓	✓	✓	✓	✓	✓		✓	✓		✓	✓	✓	✓		✓	
Engineering works: aircraft manufacturing works	✓			✓	✓	✓	✓		✓			✓			✓	✓	✓	✓	✓	✓	
Engineering works: electrical and electronic equipment manufacturing works (including works manufacturing equipment containing PCBs)	✓		✓	✓	✓	✓	✓	✓	✓	✓		✓	✓		✓	✓	✓	✓		✓	✓
Engineering works: mechanical engineering and ordnance works	✓			✓	✓	✓	✓	✓	✓		✓			✓	✓	✓		✓	✓		✓
Engineering works: railway engineering works	✓				✓	✓	✓	✓	✓			✓			✓		✓	✓		✓	
Engineering works: shipbuilding repair and shipbreaking (including naval shipyards)	✓				✓	✓	✓	✓	✓				✓					✓		✓	
Engineering works: vehicle manufacturing works				✓	✓	✓	✓	✓		✓		✓	✓		✓	✓	✓	✓		✓	
Fibreglass and fibreglass resin manufacturing works	✓			✓	✓	✓	✓	✓	✓	✓		✓	✓		✓	✓		✓		✓	

Table A1.1. Metals, semi-metals and inorganic chemicals associated with industrial uses of land

Industry (Continued)	Key Contaminants																				
	Metals and semi-metals															Inorganic chemicals					
	As	Ba	Be	Cd	Cr	Cu	Pb	Hg	Ni	Se	V	Zn	CN-free	CN-complex	NO$_3^-$	SO$_4^{2-}$	S^{2-}	Asbestos	B	pH	So
Gasworks, coke works and other coal carbonisation plants	✓			✓	✓	✓	✓	✓	✓		✓	✓	✓	✓		✓	✓	✓		✓	✓
Glass manufacturing works	✓			✓	✓	✓	✓	✓			✓	✓	✓		✓	✓	✓	✓	✓	✓	
Metal manufacturing, refining and finishing works: electroplating and other metal finishing work				✓	✓	✓	✓		✓			✓	✓		✓	✓	✓	✓	✓	✓	
Metal manufacturing, refining and finishing works: iron and steel works	✓				✓	✓	✓	✓	✓		✓	✓	✓			✓	✓	✓		✓	✓
Metal manufacturing, refining and finishing works: lead works	✓			✓	✓	✓	✓					✓				✓	✓	✓		✓	
Metal manufacturing, refining and finishing works: non-ferrous metals (excluding lead works)				✓	✓	✓	✓		✓		✓							✓	✓		
Metal manufacturing, refining and finishing works: precious metal recovery works	✓			✓	✓	✓	✓	✓				✓			✓	✓	✓	✓		✓	
Oil refineries and bulk storage of crude oil and petroleum products	✓				✓	✓	✓	✓	✓				✓			✓	✓	✓		✓	
Photographic processing industry	✓	✓		✓	✓	✓	✓	✓		✓	✓		✓		✓	✓	✓	✓		✓	
Power stations (excluding nuclear power stations)	✓		✓	✓	✓	✓	✓	✓	✓	✓	✓	✓				✓	✓	✓		✓	
Printing and bookbinding works	✓			✓	✓	✓	✓	✓	✓	✓		✓	✓		✓	✓		✓		✓	
Pulp and paper manufacturing works	✓			✓	✓	✓	✓	✓				✓				✓	✓	✓		✓	
Railway land	✓			✓	✓	✓	✓		✓		✓							✓			
Road vehicle servicing and repair: garages and filling stations	✓				✓	✓	✓					✓				✓		✓		✓	
Road vehicle servicing and repair: transport and haulage centres	✓				✓	✓	✓		✓		✓							✓		✓	✓
Sewage works and sewage farms	✓			✓	✓	✓	✓	✓				✓	✓		✓	✓	✓	✓		✓	
Textile works and dye works	✓			✓	✓	✓	✓	✓				✓			✓	✓	✓	✓	✓	✓	
Timber products manufacturing works	✓				✓	✓	✓					✓				✓		✓	✓		
Timber treatment works	✓				✓	✓						✓					✓	✓	✓	✓	
Waste recycling, treatment and disposal sites: drum and tank cleaning and recycling plants		✓				✓	✓	✓								✓		✓			
Waste recycling, treatment and disposal sites: hazardous waste treatment plants	✓			✓	✓	✓	✓	✓	✓	✓	✓	✓			✓			✓		✓	
Waste recycling, treatment and disposal sites: landfills and other waste treatment or waste disposal sites	✓			✓	✓	✓	✓	✓				✓					✓	✓	✓	✓	
Waste recycling, treatment and disposal sites: solvent recovery works				✓	✓	✓	✓	✓				✓	✓			✓	✓	✓		✓	
Waste recycling, treatment and disposal sites: metal recycling sites	✓	✓		✓	✓	✓	✓	✓	✓			✓	✓			✓	✓	✓		✓	

Table A1.2 Organic chemicals associated with industrial uses of land

Industry	Phenol	Propanone	Chlorophenols	Oil/fuel hydrocarbons	Aromatic hydrocarbons	PAHs	Chlorinated aliphatic hydrocarbons	γ, β & δ-hexachloro-cyclohexane	Dieldrin	Chlorinated aromatic hydrocarbons	PCBs	Dioxins & furans	Organolead compounds	Organotin compounds
Airports	✓			✓	✓	✓	✓				✓			
Animal and animal products processing works		✓			✓	✓	✓		✓					
Asbestos manufacturing works		✓			✓	✓	✓				✓			
Ceramics, cement and asphalt manufacturing works				✓	✓	✓					✓			
Charcoal works		✓			✓	✓	✓				✓			✓
Chemical works: coatings and printing inks manufacturing works	✓				✓	✓	✓							
Chemical works: cosmetics and toiletries manufacturing works		✓			✓	✓	✓							
Chemical works: disinfectants manufacturing works	✓	✓	✓		✓	✓				✓	✓	✓		
Chemical works: explosives, propellants and pyrotechnics manufacturing works	✓	✓		✓	✓	✓	✓				✓			
Chemical works: fertiliser manufacturing works	✓			✓	✓	✓								
Chemical works: fine chemicals manufacturing works	✓	✓			✓	✓					✓	✓		
Chemical works: inorganic chemicals manufacturing works	✓				✓									
Chemical works: linoleum vinyl and bitumen-based floor covering manufacturing works	✓	✓		✓	✓	✓	✓			✓	✓	✓		✓
Chemical works: mastics, sealants, adhesives and roofing felt manufacturing works	✓			✓	✓	✓	✓							
Chemical works: organic chemicals manufacturing works	✓	✓			✓		✓				✓			
Chemical works: pesticides manufacturing works	✓		✓	✓	✓	✓	✓	✓	✓	✓	✓	✓		✓
Chemical works: pharmaceuticals manufacturing works	✓			✓	✓	✓	✓			✓	✓			
Chemical works: rubber processing works (including works manufacturing tyres and other rubber products)		✓					✓							
Chemical works: soap and detergent manufacturing works	✓	✓		✓	✓	✓	✓							
Dockyards and dockland	✓			✓	✓	✓	✓	✓		✓	✓			
Dry cleaners		✓			✓		✓				✓			
Engineering works: aircraft manufacturing works		✓			✓		✓				✓			
Engineering works: electrical and electronic equipment manufacturing works (including works manufacturing equipment containing PCBs)					✓	✓	✓							
Engineering works: mechanical engineering and ordnance works	✓	✓			✓	✓	✓				✓			
Engineering works: railway engineering works					✓	✓	✓				✓			
Engineering works: shipbuilding repair and shipbreaking (including naval shipyards)	✓	✓		✓	✓									✓
Engineering works: vehicle manufacturing works	✓			✓	✓	✓	✓				✓			
Fibreglass and fibreglass resin manufacturing works	✓	✓		✓	✓	✓	✓				✓			
Gasworks, coke works and other coal carbonisation plants	✓			✓	✓	✓	✓							
Glass manufacturing works		✓		✓	✓						✓			
Metal manufacturing, refining and finishing works: electroplating and other metal finishing works	✓			✓	✓	✓	✓							
Metal manufacturing, refining and finishing works: iron and steel works	✓			✓	✓	✓	✓				✓			
Metal manufacturing, refining and finishing works: lead works				✓	✓	✓	✓				✓			
Metal manufacturing, refining and finishing works: non-ferrous metals (excluding lead works)				✓	✓	✓	✓				✓			

Table A1.2 Organic chemicals associated with industrial uses of land

Industry (Continued)	Phenol	Propanone	Chlorophenols	Oil/fuel hydrocarbons	Aromatic hydrocarbons	PAHs	Chlorinated aliphatic hydrocarbons	γ,3 & μ-hexachloro-cyclohexane	Dieldrin	Chlorinated aromatic hydrocarbons	PCBs	Dioxins & furans	Organolead compounds	Organotin compounds
Metal manufacturing, refining and finishing works: precious metal recovery works				✓			✓				✓			
Oil refineries and bulk storage of crude oil and petroleum products	✓	✓		✓	✓						✓		✓	
Photographic processing industry		✓			✓		✓				✓			
Power stations (excluding nuclear power stations)				✓		✓	✓				✓			
Printing and bookbinding works		✓			✓		✓				✓			
Pulp and paper manufacturing works				✓			✓	✓		✓	✓	✓		
Railway land						✓	✓				✓			
Road vehicle servicing and repair: garages and filling stations				✓	✓	✓	✓				✓		✓	
Road vehicle servicing and repair: transport and haulage centres		✓			✓	✓	✓				✓		✓	
Sewage works and sewage farms				✓			✓							
Textile works and dye works	✓	✓		✓	✓		✓		✓	✓	✓			
Timber products manufacturing works	✓	✓			✓	✓								
Timber treatment works	✓		✓	✓		✓	✓	✓						✓
Waste recycling, treatment and disposal sites: drum and tank cleaning and recycling plants		✓			✓						✓			
Waste recycling, treatment and disposal sites: hazardous waste treatment plants	✓						✓	✓	✓	✓	✓			
Waste recycling, treatment and disposal sites: landfills and other waste treatment or waste disposal sites				✓		✓	✓			✓	✓	✓		
Waste recycling, treatment and disposal sites: solvent recovery works							✓			✓	✓			
Waste recycling, treatment and disposal sites: metal recycling sites				✓			✓				✓			

APPENDIX 2. Description of key methodologies for risk estimation

A2.1 Introduction

Numerous methodologies can be used to assess the potential health and environmental impacts of contaminated land. Many are available in the form of modelling software which requires extensive or complex input data, but some are simple desk-based methods using widely available published information, possibly supplemented by site-specific information obtained from invasive surveys.

Details of the key approaches available to assist in the assessment are provided below. All of the approaches are based on the source-pathway-receptor concept for risk assessment.

A2.2 Prioritisation of contaminated sites

CLR6, published by the Department of the Environment, gives guidance to local authorities, landowners, developers and others with responsibilities for the environmental and health effects of contaminated land in deciding what priority to give to action on a site that may be contaminated. The report sets out a simple but systematic approach which allows sites that may be contaminated to be prioritised for future actions based on an assessment of the potential or actual environmental impacts.

The principal objective of the report is an initial screening of potentially contaminated sites to identify sites in the most sensitive locations. The methodology and procedures presented in the report allow all practitioners a consistent approach to follow. Resources can then be targeted at the more sensitive sites. Actions which may be indicated from the initial screening exercise include a more detailed desk top study, a ground investigation or site-specific risk assessment, or the development of a remedial strategy. The procedures make use of a limited amount of basic data and the placing of sites in a priority category is not definitive. Further ground investigation or risk assessment may result in the revision of priority categorisation. For example, the results of a ground investigation may show that contaminants originally assumed to be present at the site are either absent or present in only small concentrations, reducing significantly the associated risks.

The procedure is based on the source-pathway-receptor approach to contaminated land risk assessment. The procedure has two parts. Part 1 leads to a preliminary prioritisation of the site based on an assessment of the proximity of a receptor. The receptors are assessed under the three headings: development (humans, plants and the built environment); surface water; and groundwater. Each site is assigned to one of three groups which determines the priority for assessment under Part 2 of the procedure.

In Part 2, the prioritisation is refined into more specific categories using more detailed information about the hazards likely to be present, the pathways and the receptors. This procedure may lead to relative prioritisation of sites within a group. If there is evidence of an immediate unacceptable risk on or near the site, further action should be carried out immediately without reference to the prioritisation procedure.

The procedure is designed to minimise the possibility of a site being placed in too low a priority category as a result of limited information being available. If the current use of the site is to change significantly, for example as a result of development, the procedure should be repeated to ensure that changes to the site conditions, particularly receptors at risk, are assessed.

Normally, sites placed in a high priority category based on each of the assessments of more than one of the receptors (development, surface water, groundwater) will be of a higher priority for further action than sites placed in a high category for only one receptor.

Any further prioritisation requires subjective judgement of all the information available on the sites and should be carried out only by suitably qualified and experienced personnel.

A2.3 CLEA (contaminated land exposure assessment)

The CLEA model[27] has been developed for the purpose of calculating the concentration of contaminants in soil below which risks to human health are considered negligible. The model uses data on the human toxicological effects of contaminants which have been collated and published by the Department of the Environment, Transport and the Regions and Environment Agency. The toxicological information is also self-standing and can be used in site-specific investigations.[58]

The CLEA model uses Monte Carlo simulations to examine different pathways by which humans can be exposed to soil contaminants and a range of site uses. It can therefore be used to assess risks for several pollutant linkages forming part of the conceptual model of the site.

The advantages of the CLEA model are that it is based on risk assessment; it also specifically provides for uncertainty and so provides an objective basis for decision making.

CLEA has been used to calculate a series of guideline values for soils.[26] When published, these will replace the 'trigger' concentrations produced in the 1980s by the Interdepartmental Committee on the Reclamation of Contaminated Land.[28]

When concentrations of contaminants fall below the appropriate guideline value or site-specific criterion calculated using the model, individual contaminants or areas of the site can be considered not to pose unacceptable risks to human health and can be eliminated from further consideration.

Where concentrations of contaminants exceed the appropriate guideline value, the presumption is that there is sufficient evidence for the potential existence of an unacceptable risk to warrant further action.

A2.4 Derivation of site specific criteria for human health

Where guideline values are not available or the basis from which they are derived is not considered appropriate for a particular site it will be necessary to estimate site-specific assessment criteria, based on toxicity data and calculated exposure. Comprehensive guidance on this is provided in the Model Procedures.[4]

The procedure, in brief, involves derivation of site-specific criteria for human health. The stages are:

● description and reference of models used;

Box A2.1 Example of the approach adopted in calculating a site-specific criterion for estimating the chronic risks to human health from exposure to contaminated soil

This example is provided for illustrative purposes only. The approach and input values used may not be applicable to real life situations and should not be used without appropriate justification.

In carrying out site-specific risk estimation, a trained assessor will need to select all models, assumptions, safety factors and toxicological and related reference data with care and with adequte justification, bearing in mind the technical basis of the UK approach. This example has been taken from the Model Procedures.[4]

The site of a school playing field occupies part of a former waste disposal area from the 1930s. Elevated concentration of a contaminant (compound X) has been measured in the surface soils across the field. The grass cover is irregular, especially in the centre and ends of the pitch used for rugby, football, and hockey.

There is no published UK guideline value for X in Soil in respect of chronic risk to human health. Excessive intake of compound X over a long period is known to have a deleterious effect on the central nervous and vascular system. There are no known carcinogenic effects.

The objective is to determine a site-specific value for the soil concentration of X below which the site may be considered to be safe for its current use.

Estimating Exposure

The most vulnerable receptor is considered to be a young girl attending the school from the age of 11 to 18. The girl would spend up to 1 day a week using the playing field during term time. The main exposure pathways are considered to be ingestion of the soil, inhalation of dust derived from the soil in the summer months, and skin contact with the soil.

The estimated daily intake (EDI) of the contaminant by the most vulnerable receptor can be evaluated from considering the likely exposure from each pathway using a series of reasonable assumptions for both the girl's behaviour and the physical and chemical pathways along which soil contamination moves within the environment. For example:

● It may be reasonable to consider that the child spends 39 days per year on the playing field for 7 years, that she might ingest up to 100mg per day each time she uses the pitch for games.

● The fraction of respirable dust in the breathing zone can be approximated from a simplified relationship between climate, exposed soil area, mean wind speed, and an enrichment factor for soil texture.

Using these assumptions and the equations for fate and transport of soil and soil contamination, an expression for each intake route can be described that relates the EDI to the level of contamination in the soil. The total EDI (TEDI) is the sum of these three routes.

Considering Risk

The tolerable daily intake (TDI) is an estimate of the maximum daily intake of contaminant X over a lifetime that is considered to be protective of human health. It is based on published toxicological data from authoritative sources. The tolerable daily intake from soil sources (TDSI) can be calculated from the TDI by subtracting the mean daily intake (MDI) of contaminant X due to background exposure. A site allocation factor (an allowance for other soil sources in neighbourhood sites) is not considered appropriate in this case.

Deriving the site specific assessment criterion

The site specific assessment criterion for contaminant X can now be obtained by solving the equations to find the value for the soil concentration at the assumed point where TDSI = TEDI. Where the site-specific assessment criterion is exceeded, further action is necessary since the TEDI will exceed the TDSI. It is of course important to consider the significance of the distribution of the contamination across the pitch and to take into account the presence of significant hot spots that might for example pose an acute risk.

- description of all relevant pollution linkages and justification for any assumptions made;

- identification of appropriate toxicological and related effects data;

- calculation of estimated daily intake (EDI) of each contaminant via each pollution linkage, expressed in terms of an unknown concentration of X in the soil;

- calculation of the total estimated daily intake from site soils (TEDI);

- identification of the tolerable daily soil intake (TDSI) taking into account data on background and tolerable daily intakes, possible intakes from other soils (off-site) and different types of toxic effect; and

- setting TEDIss equal to TDSI and calculation of the critical soil concentration value (CSCrit), which is then designated as the site specific assessment criterion, which is used in the same way as the generic criteria (that is the guideline values).

The example in Box A2.1 illustrates this approach.

A2.5 Derivation of remedial targets for soil and groundwater to protect water resources

The environment agencies have developed a standardised, practical and reasonable approach to soil and groundwater remediation for the protection of water resources that can be applied on a site-by-site basis and is consistent with current legislation and guidance. The approach is described in an Environment Agency report on a *Methodology for the Derivation of Remedial Targets for Soil and Groundwater to Protect Water Resources*[59].

This report provides a methodology to derive the level of remediation required to protect groundwater and surface water. It forms part of the overall process to evaluate the health and environmental risk that contaminated soil and groundwater represents. The methodology is based on a *risk assessment* approach incorporating a *source-pathway-receptor* analysis, that leads to the derivation of site-specific remediation criteria based on an assessment of the potential impact at the identified receptor.

Consistent with the environment agencies' approach to risk assessment, the overall methodology adopts a tiered approach to determine risk-based remedial targets for soil and groundwater, involving structured decision-making, cost-benefit considerations and progressive data collection and analysis. At each tier a remedial target is derived, but this is likely to be less onerous at the next tier as additional processes (such as dilution and degradation) which affect contaminant concentrations along its pathway to the receptor, are taken into account. With successive tiers, the data requirements and the sophistication of the analysis increase, and the confidence in the predicted impact also increases. Consequently the source-pathway-receptor relationship is better defined and remedial requirements are likely to be less onerous, if the risk assessment is favourable. The tiered approach enables low risk sites to be screened out and attention to be focused on those sites where the risks to the water are greatest.

The principal objectives are to determine which of the following are required:

- no remedial action, that is, the level of contamination does not or is not likely to cause pollution of surface water or groundwater;

- remedial action to protect an identified groundwater or surface water receptor;

- further analysis and data collection to quantify the degree of risk to the receptor.

The report provides guidance on assessing and managing risks associated with contaminated groundwater and should be read before, and used in conjunction with new software tools such as the software package ConSim, which has been produced for the Environment Agency to assist in the probabilistic modelling of risks to controlled waters from land contamination.[41]

A2.6 The ConSim model

This software is described in the Environment Agency manual on CONSIM (*Contamination Impact on Groundwater: Simulation by Monte Carlo Method*)[41], produced through Environment Agency R&D programme. The model has been developed on behalf of the Environment Agency to provide those concerned with the management of contaminated land with a means of assessing the risk posed to groundwater by leaching contaminants.

The software models contaminant mobilisation and transport and is intended to use commonly available ground investigation data. The calculations performed in ConSim use the same analytical solutions to groundwater flow and contaminant transport equations employed in the *Methodology for the Derivation of Remedial Targets for Soil and Groundwater to Protect Water Resources*[59] but, where appropriate, these are coupled with probabilistic Monte Carlo simulations. The probabilistic methodology allows full incorporation of data uncertainty so that the assessment may be rational and consistent. ConSim has been designed specifically to assess the impact of contaminant migration on groundwater although it does not model the detailed physical, chemical and biological processes that can influence contaminant mobilisation, migration, retardation and attenuation. It cannot be used to assess the impact by soil contamination on any receptor other than controlled waters.

- The issues that can be addressed using ConSim include the following:

- the plausibility of a significant pollutant linkage existing for a site with respect to its potential to cause pollution of controlled waters;

- whether the collection of additional ground investigation data is required in order to quantify the risk to groundwater posed by the land contamination;

- determination of the extent of remediation required in order to reduce the risk of contamination of controlled waters to an acceptable level;

- comparison of the viability of various remedial techniques to reduce the risks of pollution to controlled waters;

- assessment of the concentration of contaminants within the source, at the base of the unsaturated zone, within the aquifer and at a receptor.

ConSim is one of a number of methods that can be used and the analyst should ensure that they are using the most appropriate tool from those available. ConSim and other models or analytical package should always be regarded as a tool in the assessment process. Professional judgement will always be necessary to integrate the results from these tools with other technical and professional guidance, cost-benefit considerations and policy, planning and legislative requirements.

A2.7 Other risk assessment tools

The Environment Agencies and the DETR have developed risk assessment tools applicable to the UK which are CLEA, ConSim, and *Methodology for the derivation of remedial targets for soil and groundwater to protect water resources*. Otmher risk assessment models and tools are also available, such as Risk*Assistant, Risk-Human and RBCA. Each of these tools assesses different aspects of risks to human health and the environment, but were developed in the US (Risk*Assistant and RBCA) and the Netherlands (Risk-Human) to satisfy local regulatory and policy requirement. They may not be directly applicable to the UK.

Particular care is needed to consider whether risk assessment tools consider all the applicable potential pollutant linkages relevant to housing developments. RBCA, for example, does not consider exposure of humans to contaminants through the vegetable uptake pathway. If this exposure route is identified as a significant pathway, RBCA is unlikely to be suitable for assessing risks to human health on land used for housing.

Guidance issued by the USEPA Soil Screening Guidance provides further information on a wide range of contaminants and has been specifically derived for residential land use in then USA. Further guidance is contained in *Methodology for Comparing CLEA with other risk assessment packages*[68] to be published by the Environment Agency.

APPENDIX 3. Model document package

The following sub-sections provide a checklist of the documents and reports likely to be produced at each step in the guidance. Outputs are indicated in bold type.

A3.1 Risk assessment

A3.1.1 State risk assessment objectives (**risk assessment objectives**)
A3.1.2 Identify hazards (**desk study and site reconnaissance**)
A3.1.3 Assess hazards (**site investigation**)
A3.1.4 State the effects of the nature and extent of hazardous conditions (**risk estimation and evaluation**)

A3.2 Risk management

A3.2.1 State risk management objectives (**risk management objectives**)
A3.2.2 Review available data from A3.1 above
A3.2.3 Identify potential remedial options
A3.2.4 Carry out a detailed analysis of each remedial option
A3.2.5 Select preferred strategy (**risk management strategy**)
A3.2.6 Design and procure the remediation process (**remediation method statement**)

A3.3 Validation

A3.3.1 State verification objectives (**verification objectives**)
A3.3.2 Record the implementation and verification of the remediation process (**remediation report**)
A3.3.3 Record ongoing monitoring and maintenance (**monitoring report**)

APPENDIX 4. Background information on key contaminants

Contaminant	Sources	Receptors					Affected by	
		Humans	Water	Plants	Other	Occurs naturally	pH	Organic matter
Acetone	Acetone, also known as propanone, is used as a solvent and in the manufacture of methyl methacrylate, methyl isobutyl ketone and other chemicals. It is produced in the manufacture	Moderate toxicity.	Water pollutant.					
Acidity/alkalinity as indicated by measurement of pH	The pH of a soil reflects its acidity (pH<7) or alkalinity (pH >7). A pH value of 7 is neutral. Most soils tend to have a nearly neutral pH. Acidic industrial wastes include pyritic wastes from coal and non-metalliferous mining, china clay waste, acidic boiler ash and cinders, spent oxides, acid tars and sulphuric acid produced during the manufacture of town gas. Alkali wastes include quarry waste, fly ash, ammoniacal liquors from town gas manufacture and certain other industrial process wastes. Acidic or alkaline conditions could be found on almost any kind of site. The pH value of a soil affects the mobility and hence availability for uptake by vegetables of a number of potential soil contaminants.	Extreme pH soils are corrosive. Risk through dermal contact and ingestion.	Acidic and strongly alkaline conditions may increase mobility of contaminants.	May reduce plant growth through increasing the availability of phytotoxic metals.	Acid ground conditions may corrode building materials such as concrete, plastics, metals, and limestone.			
Aliphatic halocarbons	Chlorinated aliphatic hydrocarbons (aliphatic hydrocarbons) are used in industry for a variety of purposes. Chlorinated solvents are the most important members of this group with respect to the assessment of contaminated land and include carbon tetrachloride, chloroform, 1, 2-dichloroethane, 1, 1, 1-trichloroethane, hexachlorobut-1, 3-diene, vinyl chloride, trichloroethene and tetrachloroethene. Elevated levels of aliphatic halocarbons may originate from industrial processes, especially chemical works, coatings, printing works, cosmetic manufacturers, oil refineries, textile and dye works, timber treatment works and solvent recovery works.	Toxic. Principal risk through inhalation. Vinyl chloride is carcinogenic.	Water pollutant.	Phytotoxic.	Deleterious affect on plastic or rubbers.			
Ammonium compounds	Elevated levels of ammonium compounds or ammonia may originate from fertilisers, explosives, plastic industries and gas works.	Although ammonia and ammonium compounds are toxic, human health is not considered a priority target.	Water pollutant. List II substance	Phytotoxic.	Adversely affects building materials.			
Aromatic hydrocarbons	Aromatic hydrocarbons include benzene, methylbenzene, toluene and xylene. This group is often referred to as 'BTEX' compounds. Elevated levels of aromatic hydrocarbons may originate from industrial processes, for example coatings, printing works manufacture, engineering works, gas works, oil refineries and solvent recovery works.	Toxic. Principal risk through inhalation.	Water pollutant. List I substance	Phytotoxic.	Deleterious to building materials such as plastics through mechanisms such as swelling.			
Aromatic halocarbons	This group which is also termed chlorinated aromatic hydrocarbons includes chlorobenzenes and chlorotoluenes. Elevated levels of these may be encountered at many industrial sites.	Toxic. Risk through dermal contact, inhalation and ingestion.	Water pollutant.	May accumulate in plant roots.	Can be deleterious to plastic and rubbers.			

Contaminant		Human health risk	Water pollutant	Plant / phytotoxicity	Building materials	
Arsenic	Elevated levels of arsenic may originate from industrial processes, for example mineral smelting, agricultural preparations and waste disposal. Arsenic may also be associated with the ceramic, electronic, metallurgic, timber treatment, textile and tanning industries.	Toxic. Carcinogenic. Risk through dermal contact, ingestion and inhalation.	Water Pollutant. List II substance	May reduce plant growth. Uptake can cause contamination of vegetables.		✓
Asbestos	Asbestos is a generic term for a number of naturally fibrous silicates, including crocidolite (blue), amosite (brown), and chrysotile (white asbestos). Asbestos con be found at many industrial sites due to its use as an insulation material. Heavy engineering sites, dockyards, railway engineering works, gasworks and asbestos factories appear to be especially prone to asbestos contamination.	Toxic. Carcinogenic. Principal risk through inhalation.				
Barium	Elevated levels of barium may originate from coatings and printing inks manufacture, vehicle manufacture and glass making.		Water Pollutant. List II substance.			✓
Beryllium	Elevated levels of beryllium may originate from a range of industrial processes. Naturally high levels of beryllium may be associated with natural mineralisation of certain granitic rocks, where beryl is the only common beryllium-bearing mineral.	Soluble beryllium compounds are toxic. Risk through inhalation, ingestion and dermal contact.	Water pollutant. List II substance.	Possibly phytotoxic. Uptake can cause contamination of vegetables.		✓ (but elevated levels from this source are rare)
Boron	Elevated boron levels may be associated with engineering works, glass works, explosives manufacture, textile and dye works and timber treatment.		Water pollutant. List II substance.	Phytotoxic.		✓
Cadmium	Elevated levels of cadmium may originate from a range of industrial processes and may occur naturally as a result of mineralisation, particularly of rocks bearing lead, zinc and copper minerals.	Toxic. Suspected carcinogen. Risk through inhalation and ingestion.	Water pollutant. List I substance.	Suspected phytotoxin. Uptake can cause contamination of vegetables.		✓ ✓
Carbon dioxide	Carbon dioxide is a gas formed as a result of oxidation or combustion of organic materials or from respiration. It is normally produced together with methane from anaerobic degradation of organic materials. It may be produced by oxidation of recent sediments, coal and other carbonaceous rocks. Carbon dioxide may also be liberated from a dissolved state in groundwater and from acid water interaction with carbonate rocks such as limestone. Carbon dioxide is frequently encountered on industrial sites, especially at waste disposal (landfill) sites and coal workings. However, carbon dioxide and methane may be generated at any site where made ground (fill) is present.	Toxic and asphyxiant gas.	Dissolves readily in water.	May be phototoxic in elevated concentrations.		✓
Chloride	Elevated levels of chlorides may originate from a large variety of industrial processes and may occur naturally.	Human health is not considered a priority target.	Water pollutant. List II substance.	Phytotoxic at elevated concentrations.	Detrimental affect on building materials.	✓
Chlorinated phenols	Includes monochlorophenols, dichlorophenols, trichlorophenols, tetrachlorophenols as well as pentachlorophenol and its compounds. Chlorophenols are used for a variety of domestic, agricultural and industrial purposes, especially the manufacture of herbicides/biocides. Pentachlorophenol is used as a wood preservative and may be found at timber treatment works and chemical manufacturing plants.	Toxic. Risk through ingestion and dermal contact with dust.	Water pollutant. List I substance.	Phytotoxin.	Some chlorophenols may permeate polythene.	

Appendix 4. Background information on key contaminants – cont.

Contaminant	Sources	Receptors				Occurs naturally	Affected by	
		Humans	Water	Plants	Other		pH	Organic matter
Chromium	Elevated levels of chromium may originate for industrial processes, while naturally high levels may be associated with ultrabasic rocks. Chromium exists in several oxidation states, of which Cr III and Cr VI are the most stable. At soil pH of less than 5.5, Cr VI is generally reduced to Cr III precipitating insoluble oxides and hydroxides. In the context of protection of human health Cr VI is the most significant state.	Cr III - low toxicity. Low risk of allergic reaction through dermal contact. Cr VI - toxic, carcinogenic. Risk through dermal contact, inhalation and ingestion.	Water pollutant. List II substance. List I substance.	Phytotoxic, although unlikely due to prevalence of Cr III in natural soil.		✓		
Copper	Elevated levels of copper may originate from a variety of industrial operations. High levels of copper may be encountered through natural geological strata and mineralisation processes. The phytotoxicity of copper is highest in acidic soils. The effect of copper, nickel and zinc may be additive.	Toxic only at elevated levels.	Water pollutant. List II substance.	Highly phytotoxic.	Corrosive to rubber.	✓	✓	
Cyanide	Cyanide can be present in soils as complex cyanides, free cyanide or as thiocyanate. Elevated levels of cyanide may originate from many industrial sites, for example gas works, plating works, heat treatment works, photography and pigment manufacture. Elevated levels of cyanide may occasionally reflect natural biochemical processes in soil.	Complex Cyanides - Toxic Free Cyanides - Very toxic Thiocyanate - Low toxicity	Water pollutant. List II substance.	Phytotoxic	Complex cyanides are reported to have detrimental effect on building materials.	✓	✓	
Dioxins and furans	The term 'dioxins and furans' refers to a group of 210 polychlorinated dibenzo-p-dioxins and furans (PCDD/PCDF) of which 17 are considered to have toxicological significance. Dioxins and furans are organic compounds produced during combustion processes and are thus present in incinerator stack emissions and emissions from burning of coal. Dioxins and furans are present as contaminants in pentachlorophenol and may therefore be found on the sites of disinfectant manufacturing works, power stations, hazardous waste disposal sites, landfill sites, solvent recovery works and timber treatment works. Most dioxins and furans released into the atmosphere ultimately accumulate in soils and sediments.	Toxic. Risk through inhalation and ingestion.	Water pollutant. List I substance	Uptake can cause contamination of vegetables.				
Lead	Elevated levels of lead may originate from industrial land uses and from exhaust emissions from petrol vehicles. Elevated levels of lead may be encountered through natural mineralisation processes.	Toxic. Risk through inhalation and ingestion.	Water pollutant.Phytotoxic. Uptake may result in food contamination.			✓		
Mercury	Elevated levels of mercury may be present from industrial processes. Elevated levels may also be found in association with black shales and from binding in organic soils.	Toxic. Irritant. Risk through dermal contact, ingestion and inhalation.	Water pollutant. List I substance.	Phytotoxic. Uptake can cause contamination of vegetables.		✓		✓

Contaminant	Source / occurrence	Human health risk	Water pollution	Effect on vegetation	Risk of fire and explosion		
Methane	Methane is a flammable gas produced by the anaerobic degradation of organic material. It is frequently encountered on industrial sites, especially at waste disposal (landfill) sites, and in the vicinity of coal workings. However, methane and carbon dioxide may be generated at any site where made ground (fill) is present. Methane may be generated from the degradation of natural organic remains in recent sediments and from conversion of organic matter under the influence of elevated temperatures (eg in natural gas associated with coal and petroleum). Natural sources of methane which may be encountered within the UK also include swamps, marshes and fresh water lakes.	Risk of asphyxiation due to oxygen displacement.		High concentrations of methane can cause vegetation die-back.	Risk of fire and explosion.		✓
Nickel	Elevated levels of nickel may originate from industrial processes. Elevated levels of nickel may be found naturally, particularly in association with ultrabasic rocks.	Toxic at elevated levels. Irritant. Risk through dermal contact, inhalation and ingestion.	Water pollutant. List II substance.	Phytotoxic. Uptake can cause contamination of vegetables.	Fire risk with dust or powder. Risk of toxic fumes if fires are lit on heavily contaminated sites.	✓	✓
Nitrate	Elevated nitrate levels may be associated with sewage sludge applications to land. Although nitrate is used as a fertiliser, elevated levels in water can cause eutrophication.		Water pollutant.				✓
Oil/fuel hydrocarbons	All industrial sites have the potential to be contaminated by hydrocarbons such as mineral oils, diesel fuel and petroleum spirits etc. Typically, these substances are found on airports, dockyards, engineering works, gas works, oil refineries, bulk storage facilities and vehicle fuelling, servicing and repairing facilities. Elevated levels of hydrocarbons may be associated with the natural geology, especially from oil source rocks such as oil shales, algal and black limestones, black shales and coals.	Toxic. Risk through dermal contact, ingestion and inhalation.	Water pollutant. List I substance.	May reduce plant growth. Uptake can cause contamination of vegetables.	Flammable. May adversely affect building materials, especially rubber and plastics.		✓
Organometallics	Organolead, organomercury and organotin compounds are considered the most important representatives of this group. Organotin compounds are possible soil contaminants at industrial sites such as timber treatment works and organic chemical manufacturing works. Organolead compounds are important anti-knock additives for gasoline additives and will often be encountered where petroleum is found. Organomercury compounds are frequently used in the preparation of other organometallic compounds.	Most, if not all, organometallic compounds are toxic to humans.	Water pollutants.	Uptake can cause contamination of vegetables.			

Appendix 4. Background information on key contaminants – cont.

Contaminant	Sources	Receptors				Occurs naturally	Affected by	
		Humans	Water	Plants	Other		pH	Organic matter
Pesticides	'Pesticides' is a term covering a variety of substances including algicides, fungicides, herbicides, insecticides and wood preservatives. Pesticides may be present at a range of sites, especially where such chemicals have been intensively used, stored or manufactured. The most likely sites to be contaminated with pesticides are chemical manufacturing works, farms (where there has been pesticide storage), textile and dye works and timber treatment works. There are over 300 pesticide formulations available for use; those specified on the UK Red List are considered relevant to this guidance.	Wide range of toxicities. Risk through ingestion, inhalation and dermal contact.	Water pollutant. List I substance.	Phytotoxic.	Some pesticides may be able to associate with concrete to attain locally elevated concentrations.			
Phenols	Phenols are common industrial contaminants, which include phenol itself, as well as cresols and xylenols. Only phenol itself is considered here.	Toxic. Can cause chemical burns. Risk through dermal contact, inhalation and ingestion.	Water pollutant. List I substance.	Phytotoxic at elevated levels. Uptake can cause contamination of vegetables.	Deleterious to rubber and concrete.	✓		✓
Polychlorinated biphenyls (PCBs)	Polychlorinated biphenyls (PCBs) are present in UK soils as a result of their use in electrical transformers and capacitors; PCBs may therefore be found as contaminants at any site where such equipment has been in use. Sites most at risk from PCB contamination include dockyards, railway engineering works, iron and steel works, power stations and waste disposal sites. PCBs are dispersed by the atmosphere and strongly absorbed to soil and sediment organic matter.	Complex toxicology.	Water pollutants. List I substance.					
Polynuclear aromatic hydrocarbons (PAH)	Polynuclear aromatic hydrocarbon (PAH) are a group of hundreds of individual compounds, of which benzo(a)pyrene (BaP) is probably the most significant because of its toxicity and carcinogenicity. Elevated levels of PAH may originate from industrial processes, for example from coal tar and coal tar products (eg creosote) at gas works and timber treatment works.	Toxic. Risk through normal contact, inhalation and ingestion.	Water pollutant.	Uptake can cause contamination of vegetables.	Although not identified as being phytotoxic or deleterious to building materials, residues containing PAH are phytotoxic and can attack plastics.			✓
Radon	Radon is a radioactive gas produced by the natural decay product of uranium. Radon can be produced from many natural strata where uranium is present as a trace element. Granites, areas of uranium mineralisation, black shales, uraniferous and phosphatic sedimentary rocks and permeable limestones give rise to higher rates of emission of radon. The depth of the weathering profile, composition, source, permeability and wetness of a soil can significantly affect radon transmission from the underlying rock.	Carcinogenic risk.				✓		

Contaminant	Sources	Human health	Water environment	Plants / vegetation	Construction / building materials		
Selenium	Elevated levels of selenium may originate from industrial processes, for example mining, smelting and refining of sulphide ores and coal combustion. Selenium may also be associated with the manufacture of electronic components, glass, plastics, ceramics, lubricants and waste disposal sites.	Toxic in soluble compound forms or as elemental dust. Risk through ingestion, inhalation and dermal contact.	Water pollutant. List II substance.	May be phytotoxic. Uptake can cause contamination of vegetables.		✓	
Silver	Elevated levels of silver may originate from industrial processes, natural mineralisation processes and in hydrothermal veins.	Metallic silver considered to be non toxic. Low toxic risk through dermal contact, ingestion and inhalation of silver compounds.	Water pollutant. List II substance.	May be phytotoxic.		✓	
Sulphate	Elevated levels of sulphate may be associated with colliery spoil, clinker from old power stations, rubble and slag. Elevated levels may also occur naturally in association with dark calcareous pyritic clays, marshy soils and from oil shale residues.	Not considered a priority contaminant with respect to human health.	Water pollutant. List II substance.	Can be phytotoxic.	Detrimental to building materials.	✓	✓
Sulphide	Elevated levels of sulphide may originate from a range of industrial processes, as well as from natural mineralisation.	Not identified as a priority contaminant with respect to human health. However, can generate highly toxic hydrogen sulphide under acid conditions.	Water pollutant.	Can be phytotoxic.	Not a hazard to construction materials in the absence of oxygen and moisture. High acidity caused by biogenic oxidation to sulphate can especially affect cast iron pipework.	✓	✓
Sulphur	Sulphur (and its associated species, sulphates, sulphides and sulphites) may be found at many industrial sites including chemical works, railway engineering works, gas works, dockyards, iron and steel works. Free sulphur may occur naturally in sedimentary rocks, limestones and around hot springs. Native sulphur, however, is unlikely to be encountered in appreciable quantities in the UK.	Toxic in excessive concentrations. Risk through dermal contact and inhalation. Combustible, giving rise to highly toxic sulphur dioxide.	Not deemed a priority contaminant with respect to the water environment.	Conversion to sulphide and sulphate could result in phytotoxicity.	Conversion to sulphide and sulphate could lead to attack on building materials.	✓	
Thallium	Elevated levels of thallium may originate from industrial processes and from natural mineralisation processes in some sulphide and selenium ores.	Thallium compounds may be very highly toxic. Risk through dermal contact, ingestion and inhalation.	Water pollutant. List II substance.	May be phytotoxic.			
Vanadium	Elevated levels of vanadium may originate from industrial processes as well as from natural mineralisation processes.	Toxic if inhaled as dust or fumes.	Water pollutant. List II substance.	Uptake can cause contamination of vegetables.		✓ (but relatively uncommon)	
Zinc	Elevated levels of zinc may originate from a range of industrial processes as well as from natural mineralisation processes. The phytotoxicity of zinc is increased in acid conditions. The effects of phytotoxicity of copper, nickel and zinc may be cumulative.	Essentially non-toxic unless in high concentrations.	Water pollutant. List II substance.	Phytotoxic.	Fire and explosion risk from zinc dust in damp conditions.	✓	✓

APPENDIX 5. Useful addresses

Association of Consulting Engineers

Alliance House
12 Caxton Street
Westminster
London
SW1H 0QL

Tel: 0207 222 6557
Fax: 0207 222 0750

Provides a free listing of all its members categorised by way of 18 specialisms, one of which is 'contaminated land'.

Provides information on enquirers of firms of consulting engineers who may provide services in respect of contamination. Normal practice is to provide names of a few firms who are members of the Association and close to the land in question. Database covers 500 different specialities including investigation and treatment of contaminated ground, water treatment, sewage treatment, hydrogeology, geotextiles and soil mechanics.

Association of Consulting Scientists Limited

PO Box 560
Wembley
Middlesex
HAO INN

Tel: 0208 991 4883
Fax: 0208 991 4882

Publishes every second year a directory of members and services which give full details of all member practices. Association members provide advisory, analytical and testing services in various fields of specialisation.

Association of Geotechnical and Geoenvironmental Specialists

39 Upper Elmers End Road
Beckenham
Kent
BR3 3QY

Tel: 0208 658 8212
Fax: 0208 663 0949

Members are both consultants and contractors involved in the geo-environment offering services in ground investigation, contaminated land assessment and remediation, laboratory testing and analysis, environmental audits, hydrogeology and pollution control. Copies of the membership list and details of publications are available from the Administrator.

British Consultants Bureau

1 Westminster Palace Gardens
1-7 Artillery Row
London
SW1P 1RJ

Tel: 0207 222 3651
Fax: 0207 222 3664

A non-profit making multi disciplinary organisation of almost 300 independent consultancy firms and individuals. BCB has an environmental group representing engineers, architects, environmentalists, lawyers, economics and other consultancy disciplines. Direct enquiries are accepted to assist in identifying appropriate consultants.

British Geotechnical Society

c/o Institution of Civil Engineers
1 Great George Street
Westminster
London
SW1P 3AA

British Geological Society (BGS)

Sir Knigsley Durham Centre
Keyworth
Nottingham
NG12

Tel: 0207 222 7722
Fax: 0207 222 7500

Learned society of geotechnical specialists. Produces the Geotechnical Directory listing UK geotechnical specialists, both firms and individuals, which is updated every two years. Directory is available at a fee via the Secretary.

Chartered Institute of Environmental Health

Chadwick House
Rushworth Street
London
SE1 0QT

Tel: 0207 928 6006
Fax: 0207 827 5866

Publishes a free directory of environmental health consultants and trainers.

Chartered Institution of Water and Environmental Management

15 John Street
London
WC1N 2EB

Tel: 0207 831 3110
Fax: 0207 405 4967

Produces CIWEM Yearbook which includes general industry information and a listing of consultants in various areas including contaminated land. See also Forum on Contamination in Land (FOCIL).

Environmental Consultants Group (ECG)
Environmental Industries Commission
6 Donaldson Road
London
NW6 6NB

Tel: 0207 624 2728
Fax: 0207 328 5910

Environmental Data Services (ENDS)
Unit 133, Finsbury Business Centre
40 Bowling Green Lane
London
EC1 0NE

Tel: 0207 278 4745/7624
Fax: 0207 415 0106

Holds detailed database of consultants and offers free search service to anyone (including non-members); searches usually produce a minimum of five consultants meeting the criteria provided. ENDS Directory of Environmental Consultants is a detailed directory of over 400 consultancies which includes information on choosing a consultancy. ENDS also publishes an analysis of the environmental consultancy market. Further details may be found at ENDS web site (http://www.ends.co.uk).

Forum on Contamination in Land (FOCIL)

Further details are available from the FOCIL web site, which may be found at (http://www.nottingham.ac.uk/scheme/research/lqm/focil.

Brings together the Royal Institution of Chartered Surveyors, the Institution of Chartered Engineers, the Royal Society of Chemistry, the Charted Institution of Water and Environmental Management, the Geological Society and the Institution of Structural Engineers, to enhance the understanding of and facilitate improved co-ordination between the professions dealing with contaminated land. Disseminates information on current guidance and good practice approaches between the professions. Enquiries to the Secretariat are passed on to member institutions as appropriate.

Geological Society
Burlington House
Piccadilly
London
W1V 0JU

Tel: 0207 434 9944
Fax: 0207 439 8975

The Geological Society combines the functions of a learned society with that of a professional institution and is recognised by the DTI as the regulatory body for geology and geologists. A directory of chartered geologists is published every two years. See also Forum on Contamination in Land (FOCIL).

Institute of Environmental Assessment
Welton House
Limekiln Way
Lincoln
LN2 4US

Tel: 01522 540069
Fax: 01522 540090

Institution of Civil Engineers
1 Great George Street
Westminster
London
SW1P 3AA

Tel: 0207 222 7722
Fax: 0207 222 7500

Produces a publication (though not updated) in conjunction with Institute of Biology, Institution of Chemical Engineers, Royal Society of Chemistry, listing organisations offering consultancy services. Information can be supplied as lists of references, external databases, searches, photocopies of articles, etc. for historical information on sites and published information on contaminated land. See also Forum on Contamination in Land (FOCIL).

Institution of Structural Engineers
11 Upper Belgrave Street
London
SW1X 8BH

Tel: 0207 235 4535
Fax: 0207 235 4294

Landscape Institute
6/7 Barnard Mews
London
SW11 1QU

Tel: 0207 738 9166
Fax: 0207 738 9134

The Landscape Institute is the professional body for landscape architects, landscape managers and landscape scientists. The Institute publishes a Directory of Registered Landscape Practices in January each year, which lists practices by area. A short summary of the expertise of each practice is included and further advice on the selection of landscape consultants is available through a nomination service.

Royal Institution of Chartered Surveyors
12 Great George Street
Parliament Square
London
SW1P 3AD

Tel: 0207 222 7000
Fax: 0207 222 9430

The RICS Information Centre holds a database of members firms and can search for those offering services required in the appropriate area. See also Forum on Contaminated Land.

Royal Society of Chemistry (RSC)
Burlington House
Piccadilly
London
W1V 0BN

Tel: 0207 437 9107
Fax: 0207 287 9798

The RSC produced a publication in 1988 (not updated) in conjunction with the Institute of Biology, Institution of Chemical Engineers, and Institution of Civil Engineers, listing organisations offering consultancy services for the investigation and assessment of contaminated land. See also Forum on Contamination in Land (FOCIL).

Royal Town Planning Institute (RTPI)
26 Portland Place
London
W1N 4BE

Tel: 0207 636 9107
Fax: 0207 323 1582

Provides information to inquirers about firms of consulting town planners who may provide services in respect of contamination. Normal practice is to provide names of a few firms.

U K Accreditation Services
Queens Road
Teddington
Middlesex
TW11 0NA

Tel: 0208 943 6840/7140
Fax: 0208 943 7134

Technical enquiry office answers specific questions/enquiries relating to laboratories involved in chemical analysis of contaminated land. Also produces a directory of accredited laboratories, revised annually.

APPENDIX 6. Summary of methods available for remedial treatment of contaminated land for housing development

A6.1 Non-technical options

Of the non-technical options, the mostly common is to change the site layout. During the review and analysis steps of selecting a remedial strategy it may be appropriate to review the zoning or layout of the development to establish whether less sensitive components of development could be placed in the areas of greatest risk from contamination. For example, where high levels of contaminants are found in areas designated for sensitive uses, but low levels are found in areas designated for hardstanding, it may be possible to revise the layout to ensure that the sensitive uses are relocated to areas of low contamination so that assessment criteria for those uses would not be exceeded. Similarly, if criteria are exceeded for private gardens, the form of development could be changed to replace private gardens with communal gardens, thus removing the risk of exposure to contaminated home-grown produce.

This approach may save on the costs of remedial treatment. It can often prove more sustainable than removal or treatment of contamination to allow the original form of development because it minimises the amount of disturbance and reduces reliance on limited environmental resources such as landfill for the treatment or disposal of the contamination.

Where changing the site layout is not possible, or changes cannot achieve the risk management objectives, consideration may be given to restricting certain activities on the site after completion of the development in order to protect residents and other sensitive receivers. Controls on construction of outbuildings such as sheds and greenhouses may be effective where there is a risk of accumulation of methane and other gases from the ground. Prohibition of excavation for swimming pools or other below-ground structures might be employed to prevent exposure to contaminants at depth in the soil. Such controls might also be necessary where the integrity of a cover system might be breached by excavation. Sometimes, a highly coloured layer is built in to cover systems to warn against breaching them should they be uncovered by excavation.

If changing the form of development cannot mitigate the risks adequately, and the costs of undertaking remedial measures to make the site suitable for housing development are unacceptably high, consideration might be given to developing the entire site for a less sensitive end-use that might not require the same level of remedial treatment. Clearly, this could have planning implications that should be discussed with the local planning authority.

A6.2 Technical options

Of the technical solutions, the civil engineering approaches have been the most widely used in past in relation to housing development. In the future it is likely that other methods will find wider applicability. In appropriate circumstances any of them could be applicable to housing developments. Each of the broad categories of remedial technology is briefly described below.

A6.2.1   Civil engineering approaches

The Model Procedures[4] identify two principal civil engineering approaches, containment systems and excavation with disposal. The objective of the containment approach is to modify or remove the potential migration pathways to potential receptors. Containment may be achieved by the use of cover systems and/or barriers.

Cover systems involve the placing of one or more engineered layers of uncontaminated materials over contaminated ground. They may be used to achieve some or all of the following objectives:

- the prevention of contact by acting as a barrier between site users and contaminants;

- the prevention of upward and downward migration of contaminants;

- the ability to sustain vegetation; and

- the improvement of geotechnical properties.

Cover systems are useful where contaminated levels are only marginally above site-specific assessment criteria. In such circumstances, a limited cover thickness of 0.5 m is usually sufficient to prevent most, but not necessarily all, contact. If prevention of all contact is required, 1 m of cover may be provided. Often, this will incorporate a physical break layer (for example a geotextile) to prevent inadvertent contact with the underlying soils. The design of cover systems must ensure that the protective functions are not impaired when services are installed and repaired. Further details on the design of cover systems is given in the CIRIA report on barriers, liners and cover systems for the containment and control of land contamination. Cover systems are not effective against contaminants that can move laterally through the ground. Such systems are not usually adequate protection in situations where gases are present in the ground or groundwater moves laterally through contaminated material.

In-ground barriers are generally used to prevent the lateral migration of contaminants. Barriers can be created using cement-bentonite slurry trenches or geomembranes. Sometimes, sheet piles are used. They may be used to achieve some or all of the following objectives:

- to isolate contaminants from the surrounding lateral environment;

- to modify local groundwater flow;

- to reduce contact between groundwater and contamination sources.

In-ground barriers are often used in conjunction with cover systems to isolate contaminants from potential receptors. Barriers may not be appropriate in circumstances where they could block natural groundwater flows.

The dwelling structure, consisting of foundations, sub-structure and ground floor, can provide an effective barrier to certain contaminants. The Building Regulations Approved Document C[39] lists metals, metal compounds and mineral fibres found in the ground which will lie within building footprint as not requiring any action (in relation to human health) because the building itself is adequate protection.

If suitably designed and installed, in-ground barriers containment methods can be used to isolate organic and inorganic contaminants in soil, groundwater and also to control the migration of gases. In-ground barriers are used to contain contaminants in situ, whilst cover systems can be used in both in situ and ex situ applications, although they cannot prevent lateral migration in either case. The fundamental limitation of barriers and cover systems is that they leave the contamination in place, so maintenance and monitoring are generally necessary to ensure that they remain effective.

Excavation and disposal of contaminated soil and other materials is currently the most commonly used remedial option. Disposal must be to a suitably licensed waste management site, or a site with an appropriate registered exemption from licensing. The Environment Agency has issued guidance on classification of contaminated soil for the purposes of disposal at licensed facilities.[25] Where waste is taken off site, developers and builders should comply with their obligations under the Duty of Care provisions of the Environmental Protection Act3 which require them to accept responsibility for waste. Waste material sent for disposal should only be carried by registered carriers. If it is proposed that excavated material is to be replaced on site, it may be necessary to obtain a waste management licence, or a registered exemption from licensing. Advice should be sought from the relevant environment agency in relation to this issue.

Following excavation, it may be appropriate to restore site levels by importing of suitable fill. In such circumstances, it may only be necessary to remove contaminated materials to a depth sufficient to accommodate a cover containment system within the planned site levels. In these circumstances it may be appropriate to leave contaminants on site below the cover layers, provided that there is not an unacceptable risk to human health or the environment. Where contaminants remain within or beneath cover or containment systems there may be a potential risk to the water environment through their leaching into groundwater.

All imported fill should be thoroughly characterised to ensure that no materials are used that may pose unacceptable risks to potential receptors. Consideration should be given to whether the imported material could be classified as a controlled waste and hence subject to waste management licensing legislation. It is generally advisable to consult the appropriate regulatory authorities to establish acceptance criteria for imported material.

Excavation and disposal may be expensive, particularly in areas with a shortage of suitably licensed landfill sites. In addition, there may be practical considerations that limit its applicability. For example contaminants may be located at depths beyond the practical reach of excavation, or beneath unmovable structures.

Development of housing on land contaminated by landfill gas and other soil gases is possible, but generally only in circumstances where passive measures are sufficient to achieve control. Where gas emission rates and concentrations are so high as to require active measures for control, the regulatory authorities may discourage development for housing.

Various guidance is available on civil engineering based methods to control landfill gas and other soil gases, for example the CIRIA Report 149 on protecting development from methane[62] and the BRE Report on construction of new buildings on gas-contaminated land.[63] Guidance on radon in new and existing buildings is given in the BRE report on guidance on protective measures for new dwellings[11] and the Department of the Environment householders' guide to radon.[64]

The principal components of passive protection are as follows:

- gas-resistant membrane;

- cavity tray seal to connect damp-proof course to gas-resistant membrane;

- services entries sealed;

- sub floor ventilation;

- cavity ventilation;

- oversite concrete or membrane below sub-floor voids

Where passive gas control measures are incorporated into housing development it will be necessary to have a high level of confidence in the durability of the controls and in the provision of long term maintenance.

Clearly, any such measures aimed at providing a low permeability barrier between the source of gas and the interior of the building will be compromised if the occupants are able to breach it, for example by installing pipework or cabling below floor level or constructing cellars or underfloor storage, or bypass it, for example by building an extension.

A6.2.2 Biologically based approaches

Biological remedial methods rely on microorganisms to carry out the aerobic or anaerobic treatment of contaminants, either in situ and ex situ. Some methods are based on providing favourable conditions for microorganisms which are already present in the soil and water, whilst other methods introduce specially cultured microorganisms. The treatment technologies are normally limited to the treatment of organic contaminants, although some techniques are claimed to treat cyanides and alter soil pH values. There are a wide range of biological treatment options available and it is important to confirm that any method being considered is capable of treating the specific contaminants identified at the range of concentrations likely to be present.

Certain in situ biological treatment methods may be particularly appropriate for treating organic contaminants in locations that are not easily accessible by other techniques, for example if they are beneath unmovable structures or at depths beyond conventional excavation techniques. However, some of the biological treatment options may be slow relative to other remedial options, particularly if they are temperature dependent.

A6.2.3 Chemically based approaches

These methods make use of chemical processes, either in-situ or ex-situ, to reduce the risks from contaminants in the soil or groundwater. This may be achieved by chemical reaction, sorption or by stimulating biodegradation. A wide range of chemical treatment options is available and it is important to confirm that any method being considered is capable of treating the specific contaminants identified within the site and at the range of concentrations likely to be present.

in situ soil flushing techniques may be appropriate for dealing with organic and metallic contaminants in locations that are not easily accessible by other techniques, for example if they are beneath unmovable structures or at depths beyond conventional excavation techniques.

A6.2.4 Physically based approaches

These methods use physical processes to remove contaminants from soil and/or groundwater. Some of the in situ techniques may be particularly appropriate for dealing with contaminants in locations that are not easily accessible by civil engineering techniques, for example if they are beneath unmovable structures or at depths beyond conventional excavation

techniques. They may be used to remediate sites which have already been subject to development. The physical methods considered in the Model Procedures[4] are briefly discussed below.

Dual phase vacuum extraction and soil vapour extraction are similar in situ techniques involving the use of wells and vacuum extraction to remove vapours, or vapours in combination with free-phase liquid contaminants, from the subsurface. The extracted materials are then treated above ground to remove the volatile compounds. The techniques are generally applicable to volatile and semi-volatile liquids in soil and groundwater. They have been successfully used for the remediation of sites contaminated with petroleum hydrocarbons and in some instances may be applied without moving structures or other infrastructure. Hence it may in appropriate circumstances be applied with a minimum of disturbance to sites that have already been developed. Limitations include the smearing of contaminants during dewatering, possible explosion hazards and operation and maintenance costs if long-term treatment is necessary.

Air sparging is an in situ technique for the treatment of volatile organic chemicals in groundwater. Air is injected into the contaminated groundwater and volatile liquids are stripped out of both the dissolved and free phase. The contaminated vapours are then collected for further treatment. In some instances the technique may be applied without moving structures or other infrastructure. The effectiveness of air sparging depends upon the local geology and hydrogeology which controls the air flow around the well head. The technique may lead to the wider dispersion of contaminants and the injection of air may cause chemical precipitation, which can affect flows in the aquifer and also encourage the growth of microorganisms. These factors should be considered before adopting this technology.

Soil washing and physico-chemical washing are closely related ex situ techniques that typically combine physical and chemical processes. Soil washing generally relies on contaminants being concentrated in separable soil fractions, for example contaminants may be bound to the clay fraction whilst the sand fraction may be relatively uncontaminated. If contamination is distributed across all the soil particle sizes, soil washing is unlikely to be effective. Soil washing plant are often based on mineral processing technologies and may include the use of many technologies, for example screens, crushers, water sprays, froth flotation tanks, filter presses, water treatment systems etc. During physico-chemical washing the separated soils are treated in a special reactor with a washing liquid, generally an aqueous solution containing chemicals to either dissolve or adsorb the contaminants. The resultant leachate is then separated from the treated solid for further processing. By use of the appropriate combination of technologies, a wide range of organic and inorganic contaminants can be treated.

A6.2.5 Solidification and stabilisation

These technologies are used to 'fix' contaminants in soil and thus reduce the risk of harm. The solidification and stabilisation can include mixing the soil with a cementitious material to produce stable solid, or the use of high temperature vitrification processes to produce a glassy product. Both approaches are typically used *ex situ*, although *in situ* techniques have been developed. The presence of organic contaminants may adversely affect cementitious processes, whilst vitrification is applicable to a wider range of contaminants. It is, however highly energy intensive.

A6.2.6 Thermal processes

These involve the use of *ex situ* thermal processes to alter either the contaminants in soil, for example by incineration, or by the use of thermal desorption techniques, to volatilise contaminants from the soil so that they can be either treated or burned. Incineration may be used to treat a wide range of organic and inorganic contaminants, but the treated soil is effectively destroyed and the residue subject to the same regulatory control as other incinerator residues. Thermal desorption processes can treat a range of organic and inorganic contaminants, but may have limited applicability in tightly aggregated soils. Careful consideration has to be given to the treatment of the vapours produced during thermal desorption since these may be polluting and can also pose an explosion risk.

APPENDIX 7. Technology summaries for remediation of contaminated land

The following technologies for remediation of contaminated land are summarised in this appendix.

A7.1 Containment
A7.2 Excavation and disposal
A7.3 *in situ* biological treatment
A7.4 *ex situ* biological treatment
A7.5 Natural attenuation
A7.6 Physical treatments
A7.7 Chemical treatments
A7.8 Solidification and stabilisation
A7.9 Thermal processes

A 7.1 Containment

A7.1.1 Introduction

The objective of containment is to modify or remove the potential migration pathways between the source of contamination and its potential receptors (for example on-site users or groundwater). Cover systems are usually installed as a long-term solution (design life times are measured in decades) and must be carefully integrated with the future use of the site. The exact construction of the system depends on the ground conditions and the nature of the contamination present. There are three main types of containment, namely cover systems, in ground barriers and hydraulic barriers. Reactive walls are a variation on the theme of barriers in which the barrier contains a reactive material (for example a chemical reactant or active microorganisms) which can treat contamination that comes into contact with it. There is little experience in the UK with such systems, however, and they are not considered in detail here.

A7.1.2 Cover systems

Cover systems involve the placement of one or more layers of uncontaminated, inert materials over contaminated ground. They can be used to address the following problems:

(1) the exposure of on-site users to contaminated soil by skin contact with the disturbed soil surface which may result from activities such as gardening;

(2) the upwards movement of contaminants in groundwater or non-aqueous phase liquids following flooding or excessive rainfall;

(3) the uptake of contaminants by homegrown vegetables;

(4) the upward movement of soil moisture by capillary action following a period of drought;

(5) the migration of contaminant vapours and gases;

(6) the downward infiltration of rainwater into the contaminated ground.

Examples of cover materials include the following:

(1) natural granular soils (such as gravels) are used in capillary breaks and for drainage channels;

(2) natural fine soils (such as clays) are used as barriers to upwards or downwards water flow;

(3) soils modified by cement or bentonite are used to improve geotechnical properties;

(4) wastes such as crushed concrete and fly ash are used as cheaper alternatives to natural soils;

(5) synthetic membranes such as geotextiles are used to prevent gas and water migration.

A7.1.3 In-ground barriers

The principal functions of in-ground barriers are: to isolate the contaminants from the surrounding environment; and to modify local groundwater flow to modify and reduce the contact between groundwater and the contaminated source. They are often used in combination with cover systems and hydraulic containment to isolate a contaminated site completely from its surroundings (that is macro-encapsulation). Hydraulic containment is often required to reduce the risk of infiltrating rainwater raising the site water table as a result of the interruption of natural drainage pattern. The effectiveness of installed barriers depends on the type of contamination and the local geology and hydrogeology. In-ground barriers can be used to contain groundwater, free phase liquids and gases.

The most commonly used barriers in the UK are based on sheet piling or slurry trenches. Steel sheet piling is an example of a displacement technology where the large sheets of steel are driven or vibrated into the ground with minimal ground disturbance. Vibration methods can emplace sheets to a depth of 30m. The joints between sheets are often grouted to ensure that the barrier is impermeable. Steel sheets are generally resistant to site contaminants, particularly organics, but may require specialist anti-corrosion coatings in low pH soils. Steel sheeting is normally used where structural or mechanical support is also required.

Slurry trench walls are formed by excavating a trench filled with a bentonite-cement slurry (called a "self-hardening" slurry). While the trench is excavated this slurry remains fluid exerting hydrostatic pressure in order to prevent the trench walls collapsing (thereby allowing excavation down to over 40m). After excavation the slurry hardens to the consistency of a "stiff clay" and forms an impermeable barrier wall with maximum permeabilities in the order of 10^{-9} m/s. A synthetic liner such as a geotextile may be introduced during wall construction to decrease permeabilities further and/or to improve chemical resistance of the wall

A7.1.4   Hydraulic containment

The objective of hydraulic containment is to modify and/or remove the potential migration pathways between the source of contamination and its potential receptors. Hydraulic containment uses groundwater abstraction and re-injection to manipulate the subsurface hydrology and thereby control the migration of contaminated groundwater or in some cases non-aqueous phase liquids. It does not necessarily involve treatment of soil or groundwater although hydraulic systems may be combined with above-ground water treatment or can be used to treat contaminated soil as an in situ treatment delivery system.

Hydraulic measures for containment can be classified according to three main objectives:

(1) to achieve the separation or isolation of the contaminants from the site groundwater by lowering the water table;

(2) to contain or isolate a contaminant plume. The migration of contaminants from the original source depends on a number of parameters including contaminant type, the groundwater flow regime, and the hydrogeological ground conditions. The size and shape of a plume is usually defined by the "unacceptable" concentration of contaminants found at its boundary;

(3) to manipulate the hydraulic regime to control and direct groundwater flow patterns so that contaminant migration is minimised. For example, hydraulic measures may be used to direct groundwater inward rather than outward from a site or to divert contaminated groundwater flow from a sensitive use discharge point.

Most hydraulic measures are implemented using well and pumping systems installed singly or in groups. Where the water table lies close to the surface, drainage trenches may sometimes be used. Three types of well are commonly used: abstraction wells to pumpout groundwater for controlled discharge or further treatment; injection wells to introduce clean water and treatment reagents; and monitoring wells.

Installation of hydraulic containment measures critically depends on a detailed understanding of local and regional hydrogeology. Therefore a detailed site investigation (both geotechnical and chemical) is an essential prerequisite to installing such a system.

A7.1.5   Applications

Containment is generally applicable to a wide range of soil types as well as made ground and sediments. It is also effective for a wide range of contaminants, although under high loading pressures some contaminants such as tars and other non-aqueous phase liquids can be forced through the barrier materials.

A7.1.6   Treatment cost

Cover systems	£15-30 per m^2 of ground covered (1993)
Hydraulic containment	£1-6 per m^3 of groundwater (Europe, 1994)
In ground vertical barriers	£25–80 per m^2 of installed wall for slurry trenches (1993)
	£80 per m^2 of installed wall for sheet piling (1993)

Key cost factors include site area, cost of materials, hydrogeology and post remediation monitoring.

A7.1.7   Specific technical limitations

The fundamental limitation of containment is that the contamination remains in place. The long term effectiveness is open to doubt with very little information being available on installed systems. Mechanisms for barrier failure are numerous and include desiccation, cracking of clay layers and inappropriate designs for a specific site.

A7.2 Excavation and disposal

A7.2.1   Introduction

Excavation and disposal of contaminated soil and other materials are important methods for dealing with contaminated land in the UK. Disposal can take place on or off-site in a suitably licensed repository. The method is versatile and able to deal with a wide range of problems.

On-site disposal of contaminated soil is applicable to large sites where the placement of a safe storage facility does not interfere with site use or redevelopment. It allows transport cost savings where a suitable off-site landfill facility is a considerable distance from the site.

A7.2.2   Approach

Excavation and disposal usually consist of the following tasks:

(1) site preparation. This includes management operations such as implementing site security, emplacing containment measures, obtaining regulatory permits, selecting local haulage routes, and the setting-up of "dirty" and "clean" work areas;

(2) excavation operation;

(3) materials handling. This stage may include rudimentary measures to ensure segregation of contaminated from un-contaminated materials, dewatering, and/or recycling of materials for re-use (e.g. crushing of site debris);

(4) post-treatment validation. Investigation and monitoring to ensure that remedial objectives have been met;

(5) off- or on-site disposal. This stage involves identification of an appropriate licensed facility for disposal of the contaminated materials;

(6) materials replacement. Where excavation and disposal is associated with site redevelopment it may be necessary to import new material to replace that removed.

Planning of excavation and disposal operations should ensure that the appropriate regulatory permits are obtained. These may include a waste management licence (for on-site disposal), discharge consents for liquid effluents, permission to abstract groundwater, development of site specific health and safety plan, and approvals regarding sensitive receptors (for example protected species).

A7.2.3   Applications

Excavation can be effective for all types of ground and all types of contaminant, but is not applicable to contaminated groundwater.

A7.2.4   Treatment cost

Costs range from £10 to 70 per tonne of soil (UK, 1992). Key cost factors include disposal prices which depends on waste type, and transport distances/prices.

A7.2.5   Specific technical limitations

Although excavation and disposal may offer the potential for a "complete" solution to contamination at a particular site this is not always the case. In practice, the complete removal of contaminated material is not possible: contaminants may be located at depths beyond the practical reach of excavation plant or beneath unmovable structures such as buildings or services. Under the "Duty of Care" regulations in the Environmental Protection Act (1990) the owner/producer of contaminated materials and those who handle it have a legal responsibility to ensure its lawful and safe disposal.

A7.3 *in situ* biological treatment

A7.3.1   Introduction

There are two main types of in situ biological treatment, namely bioventing and bioremediation using groundwater recirculation. Bioventing is an approach for optimising biodegradation in soil through the in situ supply of oxygen to indigenous microbial populations. Bioventing systems are the product of process integration, combining features of in situ soil vapour extraction with bioremediation. Bioremediation using groundwater recirculation seeks to simulate in situ biodegradation of contaminants by the addition of dissolved oxygen (or another oxidant such as hydrogen peroxide) and nutrients to groundwater, which is recirculated through the soil in order to optimise treatment conditions. Treatment may be attempted using indigenous microbial populations or laboratory-prepared inocula. Other chemical additives, such as surfactants, may be added to reduce contaminant toxicity to micro-organisms or to increase contaminant bioavailability.

A7.3.2   Bioventing

In bioventing systems, oxygen is supplied to the soil using a combination of the following:

(1) injection of air into the contaminated zone with a vacuum extraction gradient towards wells positioned outside the contaminated zone;

(2) injection of air into the subsurface outside the contaminated zone with a vacuum extraction gradient towards wells positioned inside the contaminated zone;

(3) vacuum extraction of air by wells positioned inside or outside the contaminated zone.

Dissolved nutrients and water may be supplied either by percolation from the surface or via a small network of vertical wells and horizontal galleries. Bioventing occurs in the vadose zone and treatment can be extended by artificially lowering the water table. It has been reported that bioventing has been applied to a depth of over 30m.

Bioventing systems are designed to maximise aerobic degradation. Operating flow rates of air are low to minimise volatilisation, and the potential need for treatment of extracted air may, therefore, be lower than for soil vapour extraction systems. The optimum balance between biodegradation and volatilisation depends on contaminant type, site conditions and the time available for treatment. However, facilities for treating extracted air are often still required. This usually includes an air/water separator and an air treatment system such as activated carbon, biofilters, or catalytic oxidation.

A7.3.3   *in situ* biotreatment using groundwater recirculation

In situ biotreatment systems aim to supply oxygen to the soil in aqueous solution in one of the following ways:

(1) abstraction and re-injection of groundwater to achieve circulation through contaminated soil. The groundwater is treated in above-ground effluent treatment plant where nutrients and oxygen (or oxygen "carrying" chemicals such as hydrogen peroxide) are added. This process is commonly known as pump and treat;

(2) addition of nutrients and oxygen (or chemicals such as hydrogen peroxide) by slow infiltration into the soil surface via a network of vertical wells and/or horizontal galleries in the contaminated soil zone;

(3) using an engineered auger system for mixing shallow layers of contaminated soils and for the injection of aqueous solutions of nutrients and oxygen.

To prevent the further dispersion of contamination and the migration of process chemicals (such as surfactants or inorganic nutrients) during treatment, isolation of the contaminated zone is often achieved using either hydraulic or containment barrier methods.

In situ treatment can also be carried out by tilling and ploughing the contaminated soil in a method similar to landfarming where the contamination is confined to a near surface shallow layer. (see A.7.4.3)

A7.3.4   Applications

Bioventing can be used to treat sands and silts, as well as made ground, sediments and groundwater. It is effective against a range of organic contaminants. Bioremediation using groundwater recirculation has similar applications, but is less effective in made ground

A7.3.5   Treatment cost

£5–170 per tonne of soil (USA, 1995).
£15–85 per tonne of soil (USA, 1994).

Key cost factors include initial and target contaminant concentration, depth of water table and contaminated zone.

A7.3.6   Specific technical limitations

Bioventing offers advantages over in situ bioremediation using aqueous delivery systems because the concentrations of air achievable in the subsurface can be much higher than in systems relying on water as a carrier. However, the effectiveness of bioventing systems is limited by the moisture content in the vadose zone. A saturated soil zone will require that the water level be reduced before bioventing can be carried out.

Significant questions have been raised over the accessibility and availability of subsurface contaminants to in situ systems. Bioventing and nutrient addition, usually as an aqueous solution, are in competition for available soil pore space and, therefore, may be mutually antagonistic.

Limitations of groundwater recirculation derive from the delivery systems used to supply nutrients and oxygen to the biologically active zone. Pump and treat systems are limited by factors such as soil heterogeneity, which makes prediction of contaminant migration difficult on even a macro scale for many sites. A reported rule of thumb is that, for successful applications, subsurface hydraulic permeabilities must be greater than 10^{-2} m/s. Water is a poor carrier of oxygen and treatment is often limited by lack of oxygen due to this. In using hydrogen peroxide, the oxygen carried increases but the presence of iron and manganese and other catalytic surfaces in the subsurface environment promotes hydrogen peroxide decomposition.

A7.4 *Ex situ* biological treatment

A7.4.1   Introduction

There are four main types of *ex situ* biological treatment. In biopiles, biological degradation of contaminants is achieved by optimising conditions within a soil bed or heap. The critical element in this process is aeration. 'Landfarming' uses a treatment-bed approach in which biological degradation of contaminants is achieved by optimising conditions within a ploughed and tilled layer. Windrow turning is an *ex situ* biological treatment process using raised treatment beds and waste composting technology. Biological degradation of contaminants is achieved by optimising conditions within a raised soil bank ("windrow") amended with bulking agents to improve structure and aeration. Slurry-phase biotreatment uses a bioreactor for accelerating the biodegradation of soil contaminants. Excavated soil is slurried with water and mixed with degrading organisms, air, and nutrients in one or more reactors. After treatment the slurry is dewatered; the process water may be treated to remove organic and inorganic contaminants and is commonly recycled.

Treatment may often include the use of amendments such as sewage sludge or other organic wastes, such as vegetation, to provide structure, nutrients, and additional microbial degraders.

A7.4.2   Biopiles

Treatment using biopiling involves excavating and stockpiling contaminated soil, commonly on an impermeable base. The base is required to prevent uncontrolled runoff of any leachates that form during the bioremediation process. Analysis of the leachates may be used to monitor nutrient or contaminant concentrations, as a mechanism to ensure consistent and favourable conditions are maintained. A network of support piping may be installed to provide a route for introducing nutrients, moisture, and aeration, depending on the level of sophistication required for the engineered heap. The network of piping may be installed at the base of the heap, within the heap, or on the surface of the heap depending on its function, for example at the base for air extraction and on the surface for irrigation. Biopiles have been built as high as 4 m although adequate aeration and possibly process temperature control is more difficult with increasing pile height. Volatile and gaseous emissions can be controlled by collection through use of a heap enclosure (for example portable greenhouses) or more commonly by drawing air through the system. Contaminant emissions can be removed from the drawn air using a biofilter or by adsorption onto activated carbon. Biodegradation is usually carried out using biostimulation of indigenous microbial communities but introduced organisms have also been used.

The rate of biological processes is temperature dependent and seasonal variations may affect the rate of degradation. Temperature can be controlled by enclosing the pile in a greenhouse-type structure or by heating the air/water entering the pile.

A7.4.3   Landfarming

Landfarming was first used for the treatment of refinery wastes from the petroleum industry. A range of landfarming methods exists, ranging from simple to complex techniques. It can be carried out on site or at a fixed off-site facility. Typically excavated contaminated soil is spread over a cleared and prepared area to a thickness of about 0.5m. To protect the underlying soil, a liner is sometimes used to contain leachates which may form during treatment; however, this type of containment means that cultivation must be carried out carefully. In more advanced and engineered systems, a layer of permeable sand may be placed on top of the liner with a network of drainage channels for leachate collection. An additional role of a sand layer is to protect the liner during the laying of the soil treatment bed so that it may be reused several times. Using standard or slightly modified agricultural techniques, the soil layer is ploughed and tilled to improve soil structure and increase aeration. Aeration is achieved by cultivation. The moisture content can be optimised by adding water at periodic intervals and, if necessary, nutrients.

Several types of landfarming processes cover the soil layer with a modified plastic film greenhouse which both prevents escape of volatile emissions and provides protection from the weather.

A7.4.4   Windrow turning

Windrow turning is carried out on site or at a fixed off-site facility. Excavated contaminated soil is heaped on a cleared and prepared area to a height of 1–2 m. Placed underneath the treatment bed a liner may be used to contain the leachates that may form during treatment. Materials such as wood chips, bark or compost are commonly added to improve drainage and porosity within the heaps and, in some cases, these materials can be microbiologically pretreated as proprietary seeding materials. Drainage galleries may be installed to collect and recycle percolating water and maintain an optimum moisture content within the pile.

Windrows may be mixed (or "turned") using agricultural machinery or specialised compost manufacturing machinery. Turning enhances biodegradation by improving homogeneity, providing fresh surfaces for microbial attack, assisting drainage, and promoting aeration. Otherwise, aeration in the process is passive.

Windrow turning requires significantly more area than in situ treatment since the soil is treated above ground, but is likely to require less area than landfarming since bed thickness is considerably greater. Moisture content and temperature are critical process control parameters.

A7.4.5   Slurry-phase biotreatment

A generalised example of the process steps of a slurry-phase-based treatment is outlined below:

(1) pretreatment of the feedstock to remove rubble, stones, metal objects etc. and produce an optimum particle size range for the slurry process (for example <4mm);

(2) mixing of the feedstock with water to create a slurry (typically between 20–50% by weight of soil);

(3) mechanical agitation of the slurry in a reactor vessel to keep solids suspended and to optimise contact between contaminants and micro-organisms;

(4) addition of inorganic and organic nutrients, oxygen and pH control reagents. Some slurry systems may also use oxidants such as hydrogen peroxide, ozone and UV light as a chemical pretreatment to reduce the primary organic contaminants to more degradable intermediaries;

(5) possible addition of microbial organisms either initially to seed the reactor or on a continuous basis to maintain optimal biomass concentration;

(6) dewatering of the treated slurry on completion of the treatment, with further treatment of residual aqueous waste streams where appropriate.

Slurry-phase bioremediation can also be carried out on-site in lagoons. In certain cases lagoons may already be present, in which case this treatment could be described as in situ. These lagoons often contain hazardous liquid waste in addition to contaminated soil. Lagoon-based systems do not incorporate physical separation as pretreatment. Mixing is carried out using specialist equipment which often includes an aeration and nutrient addition system.

A7.4.6   Applications

These methods can be used to treat degradable organics, including PAHs and non-halogenated compounds. They may also be effective for cyanides. They are effective in granular soils, such as sand and silts, but not clays and peats. They can also be used to treat made ground and sediments.

A7.4.7   Treatment cost

Biopiling:	£10–65 per tonne of soil (USA, 1994).
Landfarming:	£10–100 per tonne of soil (USA, 1994).
Windrow turning: biotreatment	£15–50 per tonne of soil (USA, 1994).
Slurry-phase	£50–80 per tonne of soil (USA, 1994).

Key cost factors include initial and target contaminant concentration, soil moisture content, the amount of soil handling required and extent of site preparation.

A7.4.8   Specific technical limitations

Often biopile processes and landfarming may have a beneficial effect on soil structure and fertility. Windrow turning may also have a beneficial effect, especially if bulking agents are added. However, slurry phase treatments may have a severe adverse effect on soil structure since treatment is often accompanied by some form of physical pretreatment to separate the soil into sized fractions. The use of chemical agents such as hydrogen peroxide may also lead to soil damage, for example through interaction with soil organic matter which either may be destroyed or altered into potentially more toxic forms. It may be possible to overcome these effects during post-treatment where the reconstruction of a fertile soil could be emphasised.

Some *ex situ* techniques offer improved process containment over *in situ* approaches, although several USA vendors do not recommend their processes for remediation of VOC-contaminated soils because of concern over atmosphere emissions during treatment. However, the opportunity to use landfarming processes critically depends on the space available since the treatment bed is usually no thicker than 0.5m and, therefore, covers a relatively large area. Where landfarming is used without a liner it has no process containment and contamination of topsoil beneath the treatment bed may occur. In this case the soil base should be monitored for the build-up of heavy metals which may leach out of repeated soil applications.

A7.5 Natural attenuation

A7.5.1 Introduction

Naturally occurring processes may act to reduce the concentration and environmental load of a pollutant within soil and aquifer systems. Physical, chemical and biological processes may act on a contaminant to restrict its movement; disperse the contaminant so that its concentration decreases; or degrade the contaminant so that the overall contaminant load declines. The most important processes that are generally included within the umbrella of 'natural attenuation' are biodegradation, retardation, sorption, hydrodynamic dispersion, dilution and volatilisation.

A7.5.2 Approach

The potential for the successful application of natural attenuation depends principally on the nature of the pollutant and the hydrogeochemical environment in which it is located. It is most applicable for reactive (degradable) pollutants and pollutants subject to significant retardation, particularly when located in low permeability aquifer systems. Pollutants that are persistent and/or bio-accumulative, or located in highly permeable aquifers which allow rapid groundwater and contaminant plume migration, are less likely to be suitable candidates for a natural attenuation remediation.

Before adopting a natural attenuation strategy, it is fundamentally important that comprehensive site investigation and characterisation is undertaken, and that the processes are shown to be active at a rate will ensure protection of all receptors throughout, and following, the remedial period.

Natural attenuation is not a 'do-nothing' approach. Environmental monitoring of the contaminant plume and aquifer conditions during the remedial operation is likely to be significantly more intensive than would be necessary for other remedial technologies. The principal advantages of natural attenuation are low capital costs associated with treatment plants and relatively low disturbance of surface activities, which may continue undisturbed during the treatment period.

A7.5.3 Applications

Natural attenuation can be used for groundwater contaminated by some organic contaminants, heavy metals and some inorganic substances.

A7.5.4 Treatment cost

Site investigation and characterisation is typically in the range £50,000–£500,000. On going monitoring is about £2,000–£20,000 per borehole, per year.

A7.5.5 Specific technical limitations

The application of natural attenuation has been demonstrated for a range of aliphatic and aromatic hydrocarbons (based on biodegradation) and heavy metals (based on retardation). Although there is increasing evidence to suggest that natural attenuation may also be applicable to chlorinated solvents in some situations, however there is concern over the potential for degradation of the chlorinated solvents to form more toxic breakdown products. Little information is available on the suitability of this treatment method for other contaminants or the complexities of treating contaminant mixtures.

A7.6 Physical treatments

A7.6.1 Introduction

There are two main types of physical treatment. The first involves washing of the soil. Soil washing is an *ex situ* physical treatment involving mechanical and chemical separation of contaminants or contaminated soil particles from uncontaminated soil. Soil-washing systems are often closely related to *ex situ* chemical extraction and leaching processes.

The second type of physical treatment involves extracting of substances from soil in the vapour phase from soil or groundwater. This is achieved either by applying a vacuum to suck the vapour out or by sparging with air to flush it out.

There are three main variants of technologies relying on extraction of contaminants in the vapour phase .Air sparging is an *in situ* approach for the treatment of groundwater contaminated with volatile organic chemicals such as benzene, toluene, ethylbenzene and xylene (BTEX). The principles of air sparging are related to both air stripping (an established waste treatment) and soil vapour extraction (SVE). The process exploits differences between the aqueous solubility and volatility of contaminants to transfer contamination from groundwater to the vapour phase. Soil vapour extraction (SVE) is an *in situ* physical treatment process, which exploits the volatility of certain contaminants to remove them from the soil. A vacuum is applied to wells installed in the ground and the air that emerges is treated to remove the contaminant vapour. Dual-phase vacuum extraction is a variation on SVE in that, in addition to extraction of contaminant vapour in air, any free product (that is a non-aqueous solvent layer floating on top of the groundwater) can also be extracted as a liquid. The liquid and vapour phases may be extracted together or separately.

A7.6.2   Soil washing

Many soil-washing systems and techniques evolved or were adapted from the mineral processing industry, where methods were developed for separating valuable ore minerals from gangue material which does not contain economically extractable minerals. Commercially operated soil-washing systems can be fixed at a central facility or installed on site. Each configuration of plant design is based on the results of a treatability study that investigates the contaminant distribution within the soil. The principal stages in soil washing can be identified as follows, although not every step will be used for a site specific treatment scheme:

(1) deagglomeration and slurrying of soil using water sprays, jets, and low intensity scrubbers. Surfactants may be added to improve suspension of fine particles;

(2) high intensity attrition of soil using high pressure water sprays and centrifugal acceleration or vibration can be used to remove surface coatings of contaminants and fine contaminated particles from larger particles such as sand and gravel;

(3) sizing and classification of soil to separate soil particles according to size and settling velocity using screens and hydrocyclones. In many instances the coarse soil fractions such as sand and gravel are often less contaminated than finer silts and clays because of their lower surface area and adsorption capacity;

(4) further segregation based on differences in density (using jigs, spirals and shaking tables), surface chemistry (using froth flotation), and magnetic susceptibility (using a magnetic separator) may be used to concentrate contaminants into a smaller soil volume or to produce fractions more amenable to specific further treatment;

(5) dewatering of all fractions produced by separation, for example, by filtering or flocculation;

(6) process water treatment may be necessary if contamination has been mobilised into solution;

A7.6.3   Air sparging

A qualitative assessment of the applicability of air sparging to a specific contaminant can be made from its Henry's Constant which is the ratio of its aqueous solubility to its vapour pressure. The basic air sparging system involves the injection of air into the contaminated groundwater from below the water table. As the air bubbles rise to the surface there is a preferential transfer of volatile contaminants from the dissolved or free phase to the vapour phase. The contaminated vapours are collected at the surface for further treatment by using a series of injection and extraction wells to control subsurface airflow. Above-ground treatments of the collected vapour may include activated carbon filters, biofilters, and condensers.

A7.6.4   Soil vapour extraction (SVE)

In the basic SVE design, vertical or horizontal wells are sunk into the contaminated soil. Horizontal wells are used for shallow contamination problems (less than 3m) or where a high water table restricts the depth of vertical wells. A vacuum is applied to a number of these wells to draw air slowly through the contaminated soil, where it is treated above ground by a combination of an air/water separator and an off-gas treatment system such as activated carbon. Although the general direction of airflow can be controlled, for example by placing the extraction wells either inside or outside the contaminated zone, air drawn through the soil will follow the pathway of least resistance. Air drawn through the soil pores carries volatile vapours away by a process known as advection. Contaminants continually vaporise from one or more of the condensed phases (dissolved, free, adsorbed) to maintain equilibrium within the pore space. In soils of lower permeability, the volatile contaminants diffuse to the preferential airflow pathways where advection draws them to the surface.

A7.6.5   Dual-phase vacuum extraction

Dual-phase vacuum extraction is complementary to soil vapour extraction (SVE) and involves the following processes:

(1) dewatering of saturated soils to allow enhanced use of SVE technology;

(2) recovery of non-aqueous phase liquids (NAPL) and dissolved contaminants. Dewatering is typically carried out in the smear zone at petroleum hydrocarbon release sites where the light non-aqueous phase liquid (LNAPL) contamination can be present as immiscible product or as residual saturation within the capillary zone;

(3) control of the upwelling effects caused by application of a vacuum to the soil;

(4) increasing groundwater recovery rates;

Free-product removal is an important consideration in a site remediation scheme since (i) it contains a significant proportion of the contaminant mass, (ii) it provides a long-term source and (iii) removal of free-phase can improve groundwater quality considerably. It is imperative therefore that the design of a dual-phase extraction system should be such that the selected ground water clean-up criteria or objectives can be achieved.

A7.6.6   Applications

Soil washing can be used to remove a wide range of organic and inorganic contaminants and heavy metals from many soil types (excluding clay). The other techniques are effective for a range of volatile and semi-volatile organic contaminants in soil and groundwater.

(1) combination of oxidising agent, pH moderator, and chelating agent is used to enhance contaminant solubility;

(2) fine-grained particles of exchange resin are mixed into the soil slurry to adsorb contaminants. Resin and soil are separated physically (by size or density) after treatment.

Leaching may be carried out using a series or cascade of stirred chemical reactors which can be either counter-current (flow of leachant opposes slurried flow) or co-current (flow of leachant and slurried soil in same direction). The flow rate is carefully controlled to optimise the residence time for soil and leachant contact. After contact, treated soil and leachate are separated by processes including filtration. Leachate is treated by an effluent treatment system and, where possible, recycled. Treated soil is dried and ready for further use or safe disposal.

A7.7.7 Applications

The in situ technologies are effective for sandy, silty and peaty soils and sediments. Surface amendment can be effective in changing the chemistry of inorganic substances, while soil flushing is applicable to organic contaminants.

Of the ex situ techniques, dehalogenation can treat a range of halogenated substances, including dioxins. Solvent extraction can be used to remove organic substances, while physico-chemical washing will also remove inorganic substances. Like the in situ techniques, adequate penetration and mixing of the reactant or solvent with the soil is necessary. Some types of material, such as made ground, may not be easily treatable.

A7.7.8 Treatment cost

Soil flushing:	,25–85 per tonne of soil (USA, 1993)
Surface amendments:	,12–35 per tonne of soil (USA, 1994)
Chemical dehalogenation:	,150–430 per tonne of soil (USA, 1994).
Solvent extraction:	,75–600 per tonne of soil (USA, 1994)
Physico-chemical washing:	,54–170 per tonne of soil (USA, 1994)

Key cost factors include soil moisture content and the specific chemical reagent used. The gas-phase treatment is additionally affected by energy costs.

A7.7.9 Specific technical limitations

Chemical treatments are generally costly and require considerable energy and chemical reagent inputs. in situ systems require a thorough understanding of ground conditions and moderate to high soil permeability.

Some chemicals are reactive with or do not mix with water and other soil components. Where this is an issue, the soil may need to be dried first, thereby adding to the cost of treatment. Some treatments also prevent the reuse of the treated material as soil, because they damage its structure.

With simple amendments the contaminants are not removed from the soil and, therefore, remediation assessed against guideline values expressed as total soil concentration of contaminants will show no effect. The use of soil amendments is a temporary effect and will require repeated applications to ensure that pH and soil organic matter content stay within appropriate limits.

A7.8 Solidification and stabilisation

A7.8.1 Introduction

Two systems are considered here. The first involves cement and pozzolan-based systems. The selection of suitable binding agents for a specific mixture of contaminants and soil type is applied following a laboratory study. In general, this involves mixing a sample of the soil with a large number of different binders and binder ratios and investigating which mixes perform best in physical tests, such as compressive strength or hydraulic permeability, and chemical tests, such as leachability. Binder additives include Portland cement, fly ash, soluble silicates, organophilic clays, and lime.

The second system involves vitrification. This is typically used ex situ, although it has also been demonstrated as an in situ approach. It may also be considered as a thermal treatment. Vitrification involves the application of heat to melt contaminated soils to form a glassy product. The high temperatures associated with vitrification result in the combustion of organic contaminants whilst inorganic contaminants, such as heavy metals, are immobilised within the glassy matrix.

A7.8.2 Cement and pozzolan-based systems

In situ cement and pozzolan-based approaches involve the use of soil mixing equipment. An example of a soil mixing system which has been developed in the USA and Japan comprises one set of cutting blades and two sets of mixing blades attached to a vertical auger. The auger is lowered into the soil where the rotating blades cut and mix the soil around them. Solidification and stabilisation agents and water can be injected into the mixing zone. Vertical columns of solidified soil are produced as the blade advances into the ground to the maximum depth, and are remixed as the equipment is withdrawn. By carefully controlling where each column is emplaced, the area of contaminated soil can be covered by a network of overlapping columns.

Ex situ treatment can be applied in several ways. The first option is plant processing, in which contaminated soil is excavated and mixed with solidifying and stabilising agents in a specifically designed plant or in plant adapted from other applications such as concrete mixing. A second approach is direct mixing, in which excavated material is transported to a dedicated area of the site where it is spread out in layers and the solidifying agents added using mechanical equipment.

Direct addition and mixing may also be used to treat contaminated sludges and sediments present in lagoon areas and ponds. A third approach is in-drum processing which involves excavation of contaminated soil into drums or other types of container. Solidification and stabilising agents can be added directly to the drums which are mixed using specialist equipment and allowed to set.

A7.8.3   Vitrification

An *ex situ* vitrification system consists of a melter, heat recovery system, air emissions control system, and a storage and handling area for feedstock. Many of the commercially available systems are modified from the manufacture of glass. Heat can be delivered by using plasma arcs, hot gases or carbon electrodes.

A UK vitrification system uses a "hot-top" glass-making furnace operating at temperatures of up to 1,500°C for a period of approximately 10 hours. The feed material consists of contaminated soil (up to 50 percent by weight) and glass-making additives such as lime, alumina, sand and cullet (recycled waste glass). The molten glass is discharged from the furnace along a conveyor belt where it undergoes rapid cooling. Off-gases produced during vitrification are cooled from 1,500°C to 770°C by a series of heat exchangers, scrubbed to remove particulates, VOCs, and acid gases, and discharged to the atmosphere.

A US system uses arc plasma heat to detoxify contaminants present in the feed material at temperatures from 1,540°C to 1,650°C. Off-gases from the vitrification chamber are passed to a secondary combustion chamber where they are heated to up to 1,370°C to destroy residual organics.

A7.8.4   Applications

These technologies are applicable to a wide range of non-volatile organic and inorganic contaminants and heavy metals in a range of soils and sediments. Cement and pozzolan systems do not work well with peat and made ground, however.

A7.8.5   Treatment cost

Cement and pozzolan systems:	£17–85 per tonne of soil *in situ* (USA, 1995).
Vitrification (on site plant):	£520 per tonne of soil for on-site plant (USA, 1994).
Vitrification (fixed facility):	£30–50 per tonne excluding transport (Europe, 1992).

A7.8.6   Specific technical limitations

These systems may have difficulty with soils containing either a high level of organics (greater than 5–10 per cent) Low levels of extremely hazardous organics may also be problematic in cement and pozzolan systems. High levels of some substances affect the setting mechanism in each case and must therefore be checked.

A7.9 Thermal processes

A7.9.1   Introduction

Two technologies are described here. Incineration is an *ex situ* thermal technique which uses high temperatures (800–2,500°C) to destroy contaminants by thermal oxidation. Thermal desorption is an *ex situ* technique which involves two processes: (1) transfer of contaminants from soil to vapour phase via volatilisation; and (2) treatment of off-gases from the first process to either concentrate contaminants, for example by condensation of metal vapours, or destroy them at higher operating temperatures, for example combustion by incineration.

A7.9.2   Incineration

A typical incineration system consists of pretreatment, a one or two-step combustion chamber, and post-treatment for solids and gases. The highest temperatures occur within incinerator systems equipped with a secondary combustion chamber for off-gas burning. A key factor in incineration is the length of time the soil remains at the high temperatures within the reactor (the residence time). Depending on the type of combustion chamber used, the maximum particle size which may be treated ranges from 0.3–0.025 m in diameter.

Operating temperatures for transfer of contaminants depend on soil type and the physical properties of the contaminant present. Commonly used temperatures to volatilise organics are in the range up to 600°C and for mercury from 600–800°C.

A7.9.3   Thermal desorption

Desorption units can be categorised according to the heating system used, although many commercially available systems use a combination of these methods. Direct heating uses hot air or open flame (for example in a rotary kiln). Indirectly heated systems transfer heat through contact across a metal surface which is usually heated by electricity or a hot fluid such as steam (for example using a rotary screw conveyor).

Post-treatment of off-gases depends on plant-specific factors but may include: combustion at high temperatures (up to 1,400°C) in an after burner followed by gas cleaning and discharge; thermal destruction at moderate temperatures (200–400°C) using catalysts; and conventional gas scrubbers and carbon adsorption.

A7.9.4   Applications

Incineration is effective for a wide range of contaminants in all types of soil, including made ground. However, it does not destroy heavy metals and some other inorganic substances, most of which will remain in the ash.

Thermal desorption can be used to remove a range of organics, heavy metals and cyanide from most soils (except peat). In the USA thermal desorption units are often used for small-scale remediation of petroleum spills and may therefore require less space for operation than an incineration unit.

A7.9.5   Treatment cost

Incineration: £150–750 per tonne of soil (USA, 1994).

Thermal desorption: £30–225 per tonne of soil (USA, 1994).

A7.9.6   Specific technical limitations

During soil combustion the volatilisation of metals at high temperatures requires expensive off-gas treatment and the generation of alkali metals, chlorides and fluorides can lead to damage to the kiln wall. Careful control of the feed material is required to ensure that system blockages and insufficient heating do not occur. Concern over the use and sustainability of incinerators for hazardous waste treatment have been raised in the UK and the USA.

Incineration systems require considerable energy inputs and are particularly susceptible to fluctuations in cost associated with variable moisture content. Soils treated by incineration are essentially destroyed and must be disposed of according to the waste management regulations applying to treatment residues. At the lower operating temperatures of a desorption unit (100–180°C) the physical structure of the treated soil may be maintained, although organic matter can be oxidised. At higher temperatures the treated residue may no longer resemble a soil at all, but some projects report that soil function may potentially be restored through careful husbandry.

There are several specific operational limitations reported for thermal desorption systems. Tightly aggregated soils, for example, clay-rich clods, reduce system performance because material at the centres of these clods are often cooler than at the surfaces. Unless emission controls have been specifically set up to deal with mixed contaminants, the presence of volatile metals at the applied temperatures can cause pollution control problems. The presence of significant amounts of soil organic matter (greater than 5–10 percent) may be a problem, since the concentration of contaminants within the reactor atmosphere must be below the explosion limit. Soils with a high pH may corrode internal systems.

APPENDIX 8. Glossary

Conceptual model	A textual or graphical representation of the relationship(s) between contaminant source(s), pathway(s) and receptor(s) developed on the basis of hazard identification, and refined during subsequent phases of assessment.
Exploratory investigation	Preliminary intrusive investigation of a site, designed to facilitate hazard assessment and conducted prior to the detailed investigations required for risk estimation.
Generic assessment criteria	Criteria derived and published by an authoritative body which take into account generic assumptions about the characteristics of contaminants, pathways and receptors and which are designed to be protective in a range of defined conditions.
Harm	Adverse effects on the health of living organisms or other interference with the ecological systems of which they form a part. In the case of humans the definition includes harm to property.
Hazard	A property (of a substance) or situation with the potential to do harm.
Hazard assessment	A conceptual stage of risk assessment concerned with assessing the degree of hazard associated with a site or group of sites.
Hazard identification	A conceptual stage of risk assessment concerned with identifying and characterising the hazards that may be associated with a particular site or group of sites.
Hot spot	A defined area or volume of ground containing elevated concentrations of hazardous substances.
Industry profile	One of a series of publications describing a specific industrial activity and the ways in which it may have caused the land to be contaminated. Industry profiles list contaminants associated with each industry.
Non-technical option	An administrative or management response to technical findings.
Pathway	The means by which a hazardous substance or agent comes into contact with a receptor.
Pollutant linkage	The relationship between a contaminant (source), a pathway and a receptor
Receptor	The entity (for example human, animal, water, vegetation, building, etc.) which is vulnerable to the adverse effects of a hazardous substance or agent.
Remedial action	Action taken to mitigate or reduce defined unacceptable risks. Remedial treatment and remedial works are specific examples of remedial action.
Remedial options	Options for mitigating or reducing defined unacceptable risks.
Risk	The probability that an adverse effect will occur under defined conditions.

Risk assessment	The process of assessing the hazards and risks associated with a particular site or group of sites.
Risk estimation	A conceptual stage of risk assessment concerned with estimating the likelihood that an adverse effect will result from exposure (of the receptor) to the hazardous substance or agent.
Risk evaluation	A conceptual stage of risk assessment concerned with evaluating the acceptability of estimated risks, taking into account the nature and scale of risk estimates, any uncertainties associated with the assessment and the broad costs and benefits of taking action to mitigate the risks.
Risk management	The process whereby decisions are made to accept a known or assessed risk and/or the implementation of action to reduce the consequences or probabilities of occurrence.
Site-specific assessment criteria	Criteria derived by an assessor in the context of an individual site or situation, which take into account the specific characteristics of contaminants, pathways and receptors.
Risk management objectives	Statements of what must be achieved in order to mitigate unacceptable risks. These can be expressed qualitatively (for example the removal of a source of contamination) or quantitatively, in terms of concentrations of contaminants in specified media which are protective of human health and environmental quality (taking into account the actual or intended use of the site and its setting) and which remedial action is intended to achieve.
Source	A hazardous substance or agent (for example a contaminant) which is capable of causing harm.
Supplementary investigation	Investigation carried out subsequent to a detailed investigation for the purpose of refining risk estimates, to assist in the selection of an appropriate remedial strategy, or for detailed (remedial) design purposes.

INDEX

Printed in the United Kingdom for The Stationery Office. TJ003622. C15. 02/01. 74888